The Complete Father of the Bride

If you want to know how...

Be the *Best* Best Man and Make a Stunning Speech

'Essential reading, and a great gift for those preparing
to stand and deliver on the big day.' – *Wedding Day*

Make a Great Wedding Speech

This book will thoroughly prepare the speechmaker to deliver
his or her speech with an originality which reflects
the speaker's personality and a propriety to match the
particular circumstances of the occasion itself.

Wedding Speeches for Women
*The woman's complete handbook to preparing and presenting a
wedding speech to remember.*

Whether you're the bride, bridesmaid, mother,
grandmother, sister, friend or colleague, you want your
speech to be meaningful ... memorable ... something everyone
present will cherish forever.

howtobooks
Send for a free copy of the latest catalogue to:

How To Books
Spring Hill House, Spring Hill Road,
Begbroke, Oxford OX5 1RX, United Kingdom
info@howtobooks.co.uk
www.howtobooks.co.uk

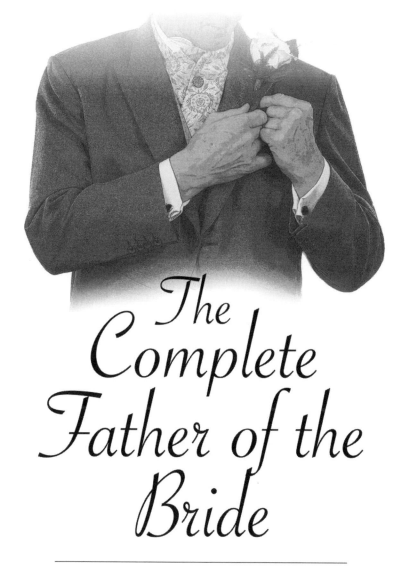

The
Complete
Father of the
Bride

A comprehensive guide to your daughter's wedding

JOHN BOWDEN

howtobooks

Published by How To Books Ltd,
Spring Hill House, Spring Hill Road,
Begbroke, Oxford OX5 1RX, United Kingdom
Tel: (01865) 375794, Fax: (01865) 379162.
info@howtobooks.co.uk
www.howtobooks.co.uk

How To Books greatly reduce the carbon footprint of their books by sourcing their
typesetting and printing in the UK.

British Library Cataloguing in Publication Data
A catalogue record for this book is available from the British Library

ISBN 978 1 84528 282 0

Cover design by Baseline Arts Ltd, Oxford
Produced for How To Books by Deer Park Productions, Tavistock
Typeset by PDQ Typesetting, Stoke-on-Trent, Staffs.
Printed and bound by Cromwell Press, Trowbridge, Wiltshire

NOTE: The material contained in this book is set out in good faith for general guidance
and no liability can be accepted for loss or expense incurred as a result of relying in
particular circumstances on statements made in the book. Laws and regulations are
complex and liable to change, and readers should check the current position with the
relevant authorities before making personal arrangements.

Contents

For Alicia. The fragrance always stays
in the hand that gives the rose

Preface

The relationship between a father and daughter is special. From the first time he holds her in his arms to the day he lets her go, their bond is ever evolving. For some, the relationship is so profound, so close, so emotionally complex. For others, miles, mistakes and memories may sometimes have kept them apart. Like signals from a mobile, they've faded in and out, now strong, now weak, occasionally lost, but always ultimately restored.

Well it's happened. Your little girl has got engaged. What do you *really* feel about 'losing' her? How do react when your mature, sensible daughter regresses into a headstrong, unreasonable teenager? How do you deal with this new alpha male in your household?

Planning a wedding can be a bittersweet experience. What is ultimately the happiest time in her life – so far – can also be the most tense. The anticipation of starting a new life runs headlong into the chaos of wedding details, family feuds and financial stress. An emotional roller coaster ride has begun.

Weddings have come a long way since the first etiquette books were written. Words like 'divorce', 're-marriage' or 'single-parenting' were never even mentioned. The traditional average family of mum, dad and two or three children no longer exists, if it ever did. Today families come in such varied structures, that more and more couples are sensibly throwing etiquette to the wind and relying instead on their own common sense.

So where does the father of the bride fit into all of this? Anywhere you want, anywhere you're welcome, and anywhere it makes sense for you to. And that applies to your wife, as well. There are so many ways you can help, both emotionally and practically. You'll find that one of your responsibilities – as important as walking your daughter down the aisle – is offering a shoulder to cry on. Another is to communicate with people, some of whom you may not have spoken to for years. Most importantly of all, you always need to be there to *support* her – in whatever way she wants.

This will be is a momentous day for you, too. Acknowledge it. Never be afraid to express your heartfelt feelings, both privately and in your speech. Don't hold back the urge to tell your daughter that you're proud of the woman she's become and that you are truly delighted for her. She may already know it, but she needs to hear it from her dad.

It's not easy being a good father of the bride, but then again it's not easy being a good father. As you get older there are some memories that will stay with you forever – the first time your daughter uttered the word 'Dada', the first time you saw her in her wedding dress – and that precious moment when she said, 'Thanks, Dad. We couldn't have done it without you!'

John Bowden

PART 1

EARLY DAYS

She's **1** Engaged!

'My son is my son till he finds him a wife, but my daughter is my daughter the rest of her life'. (Dinah Maria Mulock Craik)

No way, she's just a baby! A rational response to the big news? No. An understandable one? Definitely. No matter how old she is, you can never quite get that vision of a smiling gap-toothed five year old out of your mind. You were the first man in her life, her first hero, her first love. You have sacred memories that still linger and refuse to disappear. The first day she toddled up to you and, for no reason, threw her arms around your neck. The morning the two of you stomped up and down in that mud pool. The afternoon you lay on your backs together, looking for shapes in the clouds.

Schooldays fly by. You're on a treadmill. You're her chauffeur, her financial backer, her best friend, her worst enemy. Then, before you know it, she's waxing her legs and wearing make-up. Things are moving quickly, too quickly, *far* too quickly. You begin to worry about the kind of man she might meet. You worry that he only wants one thing from her. And you know exactly what that one thing is because it is the same thing you wanted when you were his age.

DADDY, I'VE GOT SOMETHING TO TELL YOU...
Then one day it happens: she tells you she's found a very special person. A new form of panic takes over. Now you're not worried that

she's met the *wrong* kind of man, you're worried that she's met the *right* kind of man. In a cold sweat you begin to rationalise your fears. It will never last! He's totally wrong for her! He's...too young/old/ serious/flippant! But are these your genuine concerns? Or is it your fundamental fear that you will lose her? Your memory suddenly becomes highly selective. Didn't she once say she didn't believe in marriage? Didn't she tell you she was too independent ever to marry? Didn't she say her job and career would always come first?

Maybe she did. But people change, as do their priorities and passions in life. Perhaps she really has met the man who has changed everything for her. Maybe she's head-over-heals in love with someone she wants to spend the rest of her life with. Everything and everyone else has suddenly gone down her pecking order – and that includes you. Recognise that this is inevitable. She still loves you, but in a different way. If you play your cards right your relationship can become even stronger and more positive. If you blow it, things are likely to go downhill very rapidly. Don't make her choose between the two most important men in her life. If you do, you'll probably be awarded the silver medal – at best.

Thanks for the memory

Memories are wonderful. No one can ever take them away from you. But reality is something else. She isn't a kid anymore. Of course it's not easy; you're not only a dad, you're a man. You have feelings, preferences and concerns of your own. This may well be an incredibly difficult time for you but you simply must handle them – and handle them well. Whether you feel elated or whether the prospect turns your stomach, remember she's no longer that gap-toothed five year old, she's an adult. When it comes to questions of preference, the bottom line is that hers, not yours, must prevail.

Serious concerns, of course, are another matter altogether. Note the word *serious*. If he's 60 and she's 16, then you have every justification in raising the issue. On the other hand, if you are concerned that he is not as eloquent as you might have wished, it is far more preferable to keep this thought to yourself. If you do decide to voice a serious concern, do so in a calm, rational, measured manner and at an appropriate time and place.

The role of the monarchy has been defined as three-fold: the right to be consulted, to advise and to warn. You do not have the right to be consulted, but you do have the right – indeed the duty – to advise and warn, but always in a constructive and diplomatic way. She may dismiss your concerns as groundless. So be it. You can do no more. At the end of the day she has the right to be wrong. Come on, Dad, you knew this day would come. You have to let her go and hope and pray you've brought her up well. Your role now is to support, not to criticise.

HOW CLOSE ARE YOU TO YOUR DAUGHTER?

There is a direct causal relationship between how close you are to your daughter and how emotionally affected you are likely to be by the announcement of her engagement. For some fathers this is an incredibly difficult time. Emotions go into freefall. Other dads - and stepdads – are far more laid back. They have less of a problem accepting the situation. Maybe they haven't been on the scene quite so long, maybe they are no longer on the scene, or maybe they simply have never been that close to their daughter.

The truth game

So how well do you know your daughter? What is her biggest fear, her proudest accomplishment, her favourite possession? Try to answer the following questions. You could check your answers with her, but you don't really need to because in your heart of hearts you will know whether you are correct, whether you are guessing, or whether you don't have the faintest idea.

▶ Who is your daughter's best friend?
▶ What is her favourite band?
▶ What embarrasses her most?
▶ What was her favourite and least favourite subject at school?
▶ What makes her really angry?
▶ What is her favourite colour?
▶ What is/was her nickname?
▶ What is her favourite television programme?
▶ Which person outside of the family has most influenced her life?
▶ What is her favourite meal?

Eight or more correct answers indicates you're pretty close; three or less suggests you aren't.

Protectionism or laissez faire?

Another significant factor in your probable reaction to the news is how protective (or perhaps overprotective) you are towards her. Try this little quiz and circle your answers accordingly:

▶ Do you have serious concerns about your daughter?
 Mostly Yes   Sometimes   Mostly No

▶ Do you worry unnecessarily about her?
 Mostly Yes   Sometimes   Mostly No

➤ Do you feel she is not safe in today's world?
Mostly Yes   Sometimes   Mostly No

➤ Do you feel the need to control her future?
Mostly Yes   Sometimes   Mostly No

➤ Do you find it difficult to be apart from her?
Mostly Yes   Sometimes   Mostly No

➤ Do/did you make the most important family decisions without inviting her participation?
Mostly Yes   Sometimes   Mostly No

➤ Do you try to keep her from experiencing pain, disappointment and hurt?
Mostly Yes   Sometimes   Mostly No

➤ Do you try not to allow her to feel failure?
Mostly Yes   Sometimes   Mostly No

➤ Do you try to impose your opinions onto her decision-making process?
Mostly Yes   Sometimes   Mostly No

➤ Do you check on her to make sure she is back from trips and home from dates?
Mostly Yes   Sometimes   Mostly No

If you answered 'Mostly Yes' to all ten questions, you are an overprotective father. A perfect set of 'Sometimes', or a balance of varying responses, suggests the most honest and healthy relationship between you. Ten 'Mostly No' answers may be sending a message to your daughter that you are wrapped up in your own life and aren't at all concerned about her.

WHAT KIND OF FATHER ARE YOU?

This is not asking whether you are generous or mean; strict or lenient; approachable or unapproachable. It is asking where you fit into sometimes quite complex family set-ups. For example, a child could have a natural father, a second father who brought her up and a third father who is married to her mother.

Obviously, your relationship with your daughter will be affected by far more than just your 'status'. There is no reason to expect a biological father to get on any better with his daughter than a stepfather – or vice versa. However, potentially, each of these roles does present unique problems and opportunities which will now be explored.

You're a single dad

The relationship between a single father and his daughter can sometimes be highly problematic. Often they are either too close or too distant, too loving or too disinterested, either 'Mostly Yes' or 'Mostly No'. And if their relationship is intense, it can suddenly swing from one extreme to the other for apparently the most trivial of reasons.

When a third party attempts to penetrate this love-hate relationship, sparks can really begin to fly. A once-adored father who finds a new girlfriend can create heartbreaking jealousy for his daughter. A dutiful daughter who finds a partner can cause agonising pain and resentment in her father.

If your relationship has managed to steer that tricky midway course between closeness and distance – if you are loving without ever being clinging – all may be well. Otherwise be prepared for a roller coaster ride of emotions – for both of you.

The fact remains that she has her own life to live and if she has now decided to marry, you need to support her. An extremely negative reaction from you could drive him away and destroy her chance of happiness. Mentally fast-forward twenty or thirty years. Let's face it, you may no longer be around and she may end up a lonely fifty or sixtysomething. Okay its cliché time, but you really won't be losing a daughter; you'll be gaining a son.

You're her stepfather

If the situation is proving to be difficult for you to handle, what must it be like for your stepdaughter? She may be horribly torn between her two fathers – or maybe she's concentrating on just one of you. However she decides to play it, you must go along with decisions and become involved in the precise way(s) she wants, no more and no less.

It may seem terribly unfair to you if you've been around for years and now she seems to be laughing, joking and arranging everything with a man who hasn't even sent her a birthday card since you came on the scene. Whatever you do, don't give her a guilt trip. Try to understand her motives. This is the man she spent her formative years with. This is the man she shares unique and precious childhood memories with. Children are the real victims of divorce. Perhaps this is her way of telling him: 'I don't blame you.' This does not mean she loves you any the less. On the contrary, it shows she knows how much she can trust and rely upon you. Support her decision and she'll love you even more.

On the other hand, she may have nominated you as the main man. Once again, go with the flow. Unless your wife's divorce was acrimonious and her ex did things that were totally unforgivable, with your wife's agreement, you could suggest to your daughter that she contacts him to get him involved in some way. Who knows, this could be precisely the approval she is secretly seeking. Believe me, if you make this magnanimous gesture, your daughter will shout your praises from the rooftops.

Three men and a baby

You may be neither the natural father nor the current partner of the mother of the bride. Nonetheless you were the man who helped bring her daughter up. So where do you fit in this complex picture now? Yes, that's up to the bride. It is probable that she will treat you as her 'real' father and offer you the leading role.

If she doesn't, be aware that there have been – and are – other men in her life. Respect and support her extremely difficult decisions. If necessary, be willing to accept a co-starring or even a supporting role instead.

Etiquette and all that

As more and more couples have divorced parents, wedding traditions and etiquette are necessarily being modified or changed – or even being discarded by the wayside. Tell her not to worry about what used to be considered 'correct' or 'proper'; encourage her to do whatever makes her feel most comfortable. She may well confide that she has divided loyalties, that she wants both of her dads to be involved. However, she may have no idea how this can be achieved. Suggest she divides the focus and responsibilities between the both of you. The invitations could include both of your families:

> mr (Him) and his family and mrs (your wife) and her family
> would like to invite you to their daughter's wedding . . .

At the reception, perhaps her biological father could make the speech while you act as the anchorman, explaining who's who, giving a little background about the various speakers and generally keeping things moving along.

You're divorced from her mother

It is quite possible that your daughter will wish her stepfather to be included, possibly big time, in all the planning and parties over the next few months – and she wants to give him a prominent role on the Big Day. Perhaps you are fine with this; then again, perhaps you are not. Remind yourself that she may well have very strong feelings for her stepdad, especially if he has been an important part of her life since she was a child. Try to take a positive spin on things. Isn't it better for her that she gets on well with him rather than despises him? And remember: she could have excluded you altogether.

DAUGHTERS AREN'T ALL ALIKE EITHER

In the same way that your relationship with your daughter may be affected, to some extent at least, by your 'role' within the family unit, it may also be influenced by such factors as your daughter's background, current situation and hopes and expectations.

While the following observations may not be universally true, they should provide useful food for thought. They may also help you understand her – and your – complex and sometimes contradictory thought processes.

She's adopted

The fact that your daughter is adopted generally should be irrelevant. As far as you are concerned, she *is* your daughter. And, of course, she is. However, matters may become a little more delicate if she has made contact with her biological parents, or if one or more of them have got in contact with her. And if she was donor-conceived, then this can become a legal and ethical minefield which is well and truly outside the scope of this book. Suffice it to say that your daughter should be allowed to make her own often very difficult decisions and that your role, as always, is to support, not to criticise.

She's had previous relationships

Perhaps some of her previous boyfriends have seemed a little odd to you. And maybe they have been. Remember that Elton John wannabe who wore a different pair of ridiculous spectacles each time he called? Then came that chap who spent most of his waking hours sleeping. And who could forget what's-his-name's impressive collection of Giant African snails? Whatever your views about the other men who have been in her life, you simply mustn't assume her fiancé is the latest in a long line of oddballs. It isn't fair. And perhaps she needed to kiss a few frogs to find her prince.

On the other hand, maybe you think in the past she's let her perfect man get away. That was her (or possibly his or their) decision. Times have moved on. Don't pre-judge her husband-to-be or compare him with the one that got away. She wants to spend her life with him. Give him every chance to prove she's made the right choice.

You're anything but close

Not every father-daughter relationship is all sweetness and light. Yours may be a little cool, somewhat cold, or even downright freezing. Perhaps you haven't spoken for years. Then you get a call. What does she want? Cynically, you may think it's your money. Or maybe she really does want you around during this important time in her life. Be extremely careful: the way you react may affect your relationship for life.

You might consider yourself lucky. You have been given a second chance. However, don't expect too much too soon. You have bridges to build and that takes time. Respect her boundaries and allow her to dictate the pace for what *may* eventually lead to a reconciliation.

If you hear from someone else that she's getting married, it's fine to make a brief call, send a card or even text her. Acknowledge her good news and wish her well. However, don't expect she will automatically want you back in her life. She may respond positively to your conciliatory gesture, and then again she may not. Old wounds do not heal overnight. Let her decide how things may pan out over the next few months.

We've been here before

If your daughter has been engaged, and possibly married before – and maybe more than once – it is hardly surprising if you are thinking: 'Here we go again.' Hasn't she learnt anything from previous mistakes? Is she doing this on the rebound from that last 'big mistake'?

Maybe you are right. You are perfectly entitled to diplomatically raise any serious matters of concern, especially if history appears to be repeating itself. However, if you get the time-honoured 'It's *my* life!' response, make your case *once* and then accept the fact that she may or may not take your views and advice on board. Ultimately it is her choice. You have done your best. You can do no more.

Don't allow any personal bias to creep in

You also need to consider that maybe, just maybe, this time she has got it right. Are you feeling the way you do because of *your* bad experiences? If you are divorced, you may be thinking how can anyone of sound mind put themselves in a position to go through all the trauma I suffered? While this is an understandable reaction, it is not a helpful one. Second and subsequent marriages often work out brilliantly. And, in any case, it simply isn't fair to judge your daughter's decision unfavourably, based upon your attitudes and fears.

Daddy Cool

When it comes to paying for another wedding, whatever you do, do not rant and rave about all the money you have already wasted. That's history now. However, if you have previously forked out considerable sums, it would be unreasonable for your daughter to *expect* you to re-mortgage the family home to do it all over again. Of course, you may decide to do so anyway. That's up to you. But be aware that if you do not make *any* financial contribution, this may be interpreted as disapproval.

So unless you do disapprove, and you are willing to face whatever sanctions your daughter may deem appropriate, it is better to pay something, however modest. It is quite possible that she will take this as a gesture of your support – and at this stage your support may well be worth more to her than your cash.

You're *what*?

However you react to the news that she's pregnant, screaming and cursing won't solve the problem (if indeed it is a problem). If you feel let down, disappointed, embarrassed, try to talk to a person outside the situation. Perhaps you know someone who has already experienced something like this and has come through it well. To be able to help your daughter, it's important that you look after yourself as well.

If she has decided to keep the baby and feels this is the right time to get married, respect her decisions. She's probably confused, overwhelmed and uncertain what you think of her. You need to reassure her. Tell her and show her that you love her.

It is for your daughter and her fiancé to decide upon the tone of the wedding. What do they feel most comfortable with? But however they may decide to play it, remember that a wedding should always be a happy occasion.

She already has children

Well, Granddad, you're going to have a (new) son-in-law ... and possibly some stepsiblings, or even step-stepsiblings. Let's hope everyone gets on well. Children and young people are naturally extremely resilient and able to cope with quite difficult circumstances. However, if one or more of them is appearing uncharacteristically reserved, or being simply unwilling to talk about the wedding, or even to acknowledge the existence of their stepfather or stepmother-to-be, there may be troubles ahead.

There isn't a great deal you can do about this, in the short term at least. You can't call off the wedding; you can't allow only the 'best' of his offspring to join your daughter's family; you can't get a court order to take all your grandchildren into your personal care. Tempting as it may seem to you, don't tell your daughter that she hasn't brought up her children well, or that she's making a massive mistake in bringing new kids into her established family. If you overstep the mark you could easily drive her away from you.

It's a family affair

Hopefully though, for years both you and your daughter will have been helping your grandchildren become balanced, well-adjusted individuals. This will certainly minimise the potential trauma of the gathering of clans. If you haven't been as supportive as you could have been, please start now. The following strategies really do help children face challenging situations, such as this one.

▶ Provide a safe, nurturing environment.
▶ Spend time listening to and playing with them.
▶ Teach them how to communicate.
▶ Allow them to make mistakes.
▶ Involve them in day-to-day activities and routines.
▶ Trust and value them.

Let your grandchildren know you support them and that you'll always be there for them – if and when they want you. But never take *their* sides against *his* children. Let the extended family have no doubt that you care about everyone's wellbeing.

She's going to live with him first

You may have religious or other moral objections to this. Or maybe it's simply a generation gap issue. The fact is though that more and more couples are co-habiting before getting married (if indeed they will ever get married at all). What used to be frowned upon in your youth has now become almost the norm.

Perhaps your daughter has told you she is going to move in with her fiancé during the engagement, or perhaps she is already co-habiting with him. Either way, that's their choice. Some people will argue the benefits of this arrangement. You get to know each others faults and foibles and, if they can't be modified, or you simply can't accept them, at least you have found out before it's too late. They will certainly have to get to grips with budgeting and all the financial implications of living as a couple. And it will be far less stressful to return to an established home immediately after the honeymoon rather than then having to set one up from scratch.

Marriage v Co-habitation

However, if they are getting married after having lived together for a long time, you are entitled to tactfully enquire why. Perhaps it is 'for the children's sake'. Perhaps it is to show their commitment to one another. But why now? If things have been a little – or very – rocky between them recently, they may not be marrying for the right reasons. If their relationship has started to lose its initial allure, they may have decided that getting married would be a way to stabilise it. This is over simplistic. If neither partner changes, the relationship will continue to decay, whether they are wearing wedding rings or not.

The other potential problem with people marrying after a medium- or long-term period of co-habitation is the fundamental change in the underlying bases of the respective relationships. The people involved may be the same but the rules of the game will have altered significantly. Co-habitation starts from the assumption of a *conditional arrangement*: I'll stay as long as it suits both of us. It is then all too easy for one or both partners to behave in ways which manipulate the other person into staying.

Marriage, on the other hand, starts from the assumption of an *unconditional promise*: 'till death us do part. The resultant behaviours are based upon the expectation of each partner that the other person is trustworthy. In theory, at least, there is far less manipulation involved. However, if neither partner adapts to the new basis, or if only one does, there will be serious and negative repercussions. And the longer the period of co-habitation, the more entrenched the old ways of behaving will be, and the harder to change.

Be realistic yet diplomatic

Of course, this is not to say marriages can and do flourish after a long period of living together. Research shows that children are far more likely to remain healthy and to achieve when part of a legalised family unit. However, the statistics are against your daughter and son-in-law's long-term prospects when compared to couples who do not co-habitate first. And most studies confirm that co-habitation before marriage – especially over a significant period – indicates that relationships are less, not more, stable.

So how do you respond to their news? As always, sensitively and judiciously. Ask your daughter why she has decided to get married at this stage of their long-term relationship. Point out the reasons why divorce rates are higher among couples who have lived together first. Of course, it can work out, but both she and her fiancé will have to work incredibly hard if they are going to successfully adapt to this new and unconditional promise. Make your points clearly and concisely – and make them just once. Speak now and then forever hold your peace.

Is this my daughter?

Don't be surprised if your calm, mature, responsible daughter occasionally regresses into being a brattish teenager. The paradox is that this regression is actually in the service of independence. There is also an expectation that this time is supposed to be so happy, so wonderful. Yet in reality she will find it is fraught with ambivalence. Is it really surprising then if she loses the plot every now and then?

The process of getting married is rife with difficulties, as many issues collide during the socially sanctioned status of in-betweenness that is known as *the engagement*. During this concentrated period of time, it's perfectly natural for a bride-to-be to let off a little steam when the pressure of wedding planning gets too much. Try not to take this to heart. Normal service will be resumed – eventually.

Peer and media pressure

A decade ago, weddings were far less complicated affairs, largely due to the fact that couples did not have as many choices as they do today. Now there is a whole new wedding industry out there, all geared up to pressurise your daughter to settle for nothing but the best. Each supplier will try to make her feel that the success of the wedding somehow rests on acquiring their most expensive product.

Images of celebrity weddings in newspapers and magazines have reinforced this message and a new condition, known as *Competitive Wedding Syndrome*, is sweeping the nation. A recent survey revealed that 59% of brides wanted guests to rate their wedding as the best they had ever attended, while only a romantic 26% wanted the occasion to show their friends and relatives how much in love they were.

We'll return to this syndrome – and how it can be treated – later. At this stage, just be aware that Bridezilla can be shown that it's the thought and personality that's put into the wedding, rather than the amount of the cash thrown at it, that will make her Big Day unique, personal and memorable.

Your Future **2** Son-in-Law

'He's like you dad, except he's brilliant.' (Kimberley Williams in *Father of the Bride*)

There was a time – only a few generations ago – when it was traditional for every prospective son-in-law to pay a visit to his girlfriend's father to formally ask permission to marry.

Although this custom continues, it is not nearly as common as it once was. Today, when a man asks his girlfriend's father for her hand, he does so more out of respect than anything else. Generally, both the father and the boyfriend are aware that, approval or no approval, if they truly want to be married, there's little to stop them. The father's consent is almost expected.

BEING ASKED FOR YOUR PERMISSION

You've probably known your daughter's husband-to-be for some time. If he's been the only man in her life for years, the news couldn't have been that unexpected. But if things didn't seem to have been that serious – and you weren't given any clues that things had moved on so much – you may well have just thought of him as *the* boyfriend, or even *a* (current) boyfriend. In this eventuality, the engagement must have come as a bolt from the blue. And if you've only just met him – or even been made aware of his existence – then you were probably totally shell-shocked by their life-changing announcement.

Obviously it's easier if you've met before. However, even if you already know each other – and you've been getting on really well – this is a very different situation for both of you. You know it and he knows it. He realises he's now under a different kind of scrutiny.

Remind yourself that this man is probably extremely nervous. He could have taken the easy way out by leaving it to your daughter to break the news to you, by emailing you (not an uncommon practice today), or by simply not telling you at all. It is brave of him to speak to you face-to-face. Respect him for this.

Put yourself in his shoes
What did you feel like when you first met your wife's father? How did he treat you? How did you feel during and after that initial encounter? What lessons can you learn from your experiences all those years ago, now the roles are reversed? Don't make the same mistakes as *your* father-in-law.

Whatever the circumstances, the fact is your daughter has found the man she loves and wants to marry. However you feel about it, be careful not to say or do anything on the spur of the moment that you may later regret. And always follow the legal maxim: he's innocent until proved guilty.

HOLDING YOUR TONGUE
If the news came as a total surprise to you – not easy, I know – unless you have nice things to say, it is better not to say anything. The time will come when it is appropriate to express your doubts, or at least ask some highly probing questions – and that time will come very soon – but you should never do this in the heat of the moment. Play for time. Be truthful: tell him you need some time to think about the situation and to talk to your daughter and wife.

It's not only what you say, it's how you say it

Of course, if you know he's been doing unacceptable things behind your daughter's back, such as dealing in drugs, having an affair, being a serial fiancé who has already been engaged to – and then split up from – numerous other girls, you have every right and reason to confront him here and now. In all other circumstances, give yourself time to compose yourself and reflect upon the overall situation. Bite your lip and bide your time.

However, if you were expecting this conversation and you have already coolly and rationally considered precisely *what* you intend to say and *how* you intend to say it, then do so now – logically, calmly and diplomatically. Choose your words with extreme care. This conversation will affect your future relationship with your prospective son-in-law – and your future relationship with your daughter.

NOT MAKING COMPARISONS

Maybe you already have a wonderful son and/or a brilliant son-in-law. How can this man possibly emulate their exalted standards? The short answer is: he shouldn't be expected to. It simply isn't fair to compare people in this way. Everyone is different. Everyone has strengths – and weaknesses.

To you his weaknesses may already seem all too obvious. Don't dwell on them. In any case, there may be valid reasons or explanations for his apparent shortcomings. They may well reveal themselves over the weeks and months ahead. Don't jump to conclusions and give him plenty of time and opportunity to display his undoubted hidden strengths. Give him a chance. In fact, give him *every* chance.

Reserving judgment

If you make a snap judgement now, quite simply you may be wrong. Are you looking for problems with him rather than being open-minded? If so, how are you going to react when the nicer, more considerate side of his personality begins to shine through? Will you apologise? Will you keep up the pretence that you don't like him? Or will you tell everyone that you really liked him all the time? Even if you have doubts – unless they are major ones – it is far better to reserve judgment until you really get to know him.

Being consistent

It is perfectly understandable that in many ways you still see your daughter as your 'little girl'. But is it really fair to consider her in this way, yet to expect her fiancé to be a fully mature man? No, it isn't. True, he is not a child but he doesn't have the same life experiences and skills that you have acquired over the years. Speak to him in an adult manner, but do not expect the maturity of response that you would from a person of more advanced years.

That said, of course, it is your right – indeed your duty – to raise any serious doubts and issues with him. Ask pertinent questions, but not in a Gestapo-like fashion. Listen to his responses. Give advice, not instruction. Who knows, he may not have anyone else to turn to and may actually appreciate your input. Make your points clearly and unambiguously but do not repeat them over and over again. If you do, he will feel as if he is being lectured and will react accordingly. If you are heavy-handed it is likely that will turn him – and your daughter – away.

ASKING THE BIG QUESTIONS

You may already know a great deal about your prospective son-in-law. If you don't, then ask. Use open-ended questions and listen carefully to his responses. Remember that this should be a conversation, not an interview or interrogation, so encourage him to ask you questions too. Embrace them and answer them truthfully.

To begin with, keep things fairly light but don't make jokes at his expense. This could well be one of the most important days of his life so far. Don't undermine him or the occasion. Once you have established a friendly or at least a cordial atmosphere, concentrate on the 'big questions', such as:

▶ What are your goals in life?
▶ What are your views on marriage?
▶ Do you intend to raise a family?
▶ Where do you intend to live?
▶ How are you going to support yourselves financially?

You may get full, frank and considered answers to these questions which will help you get a better picture of how things are likely to pan out. Alternatively, you may just get blank looks. If he hasn't even thought about these things before, he may at least start thinking about them now.

Then return to lighter topics. Talk about his job, hobbies and interests. This encounter is all about effective communication. The word 'communication' comes from the Latin *communicare*, which means 'to share'. In other words, this should be a two-way process. So, if he seems interested, tell him about *your* job, hobbies and interests.

Watching your (body) language

As you talk, continually ask yourself: what does he make of *me*? What hidden, possibly unintentional messages might you be sending out? I'm sure you can imagine what his reaction would be if you continually glare at him, arms crossed, or if you stare blankly out of the window, finger-tapping the table, as he tries to put into words his heartfelt feelings towards your daughter. He could even feel intimidated if you are wearing your Sunday best while he is in tee-shirt and trainers. Take off your jacket and loosen or remove your tie. Help him feel at ease.

You are almost certainly of different generations with different and sometimes opposing expectations and values. It is hardly surprising if you have very different outlooks on life. The key is to find common ground and to build upon it as you seek mutually acceptable compromises to fundamental differences.

BEING OPEN MINDED

Everyone has a past. By all means look for trends and patterns which could easily repeat themselves in the future. Is he giving you *excuses* or genuine *reasons* why things have not always gone as smoothly as he would have hoped? However, also be aware that people do change, mature and learn from their previous mistakes. Give him a chance.

So what is his background? Why does he want to marry your daughter? What are his – and their – hopes and fears? Big questions that require truthful answers.

He's been married before

Perhaps he's been married before or he's been in a long-term relationship with someone other than your daughter. How do you handle that? Well first be reassured that this is a far from an unusual situation nowadays. You are perfectly entitled to ask him about how and why things have gone wrong before.

However, unless you are aware of any serious reasons for the breakdown of previous relationships (perhaps physical abuse or substance abuse), you should not form any snap judgments as to his suitability. Sometimes it's difficult, but you really must give him every chance. Okay, he may have made mistakes and taken wrong decisions in the past (haven't we all?). Maybe he knows what he's doing this time around.

He's already got children

If he has children in tow from one or more previous relationships, you are going to become an instant (step-) grandfather. However, you may feel about this, remember that your daughter has accepted – or even embraced – the situation. So should you.

His children may well already have one or two sets of grandparents. So precisely where will you fit in? Only time will tell. It's up to them, as well as to you. You may all hit it off brilliantly from Day One. Children certainly aren't limited to accepting love from blood relatives. And who knows, if you treat these children as part of your family, you may find you are seeing far more of your daughter and finding your relationship with her growing even stronger.

Taking it on the chin

Then again, things may not run so smoothly. Teenage children in particular can have massive hang-ups about re-marriages. If they don't like the situation – and even if they become verbally abusive to you – paradoxically, you really shouldn't take it personally. It is your role they are uncomfortable with, it's not you as a person. And never react in kind or expect them to accept you. In time they may come around – or they may not. Just let them know you will always be there for them, if and when they want you.

Of course his children may well be with their biological mother(s). Obviously your daughter should be made fully aware of any financial commitment your future son-in-law has to support them.

Love on the dole?

If he hasn't got a penny to his name, your first reaction will probably be: don't marry my daughter, or at least postpone the wedding until you can support *yourself*. Understandably, you would also have serious doubts if your daughter (and you) are well off and this impoverished person seems to have materialised out of nowhere.

But there may be genuine reasons for his (hopefully temporary) financial embarrassment. There is a big difference between a man who has just worked his way through university and another who has spent the last five years sitting at home, all day, everyday, sending off scripts to Hollywood film producers in the vague hope that one day one of them may be accepted.

Getting your priorities right

Perhaps he's never lived independently before and he's broke because nothing but the latest (and most expensive) iPod, iPhone, PSP, Nintendo Wii and DS Lite will do. If this is the case, he needs a serious reality check. Don't be aggressive, but point out that he should have other priorities in life, especially now he's intending to get married. Talk him through monthly income and monthly expenditure. Show him some typical utility bills.

You could offer to accept money from him each month and deal with his bills, at least until he gets on a more sound financial footing. Or you may decide to give him (or better, them) a financial loan or gift. Then again, you may decide to offer them some temporary accommodation either now or after the wedding.

He's homeless

It's not ideal to start married life under the same roof as your parents(-in-law). But it's a lot better than starting out under no roof at all. From your point of view though, before you make any rash offers or promises, it is prudent to think about things very carefully and to talk them through with your wife. You may love the idea of a two or even three generation household. But is this really because you would be postponing the inevitable day when your daughter finally leaves the nest?

Remember that everyone needs their space. Would there be adequate room for you all? Even if physical space is not an issue, is it likely that the four of you – and any other offspring already living there and/or moving in with the newlyweds – *all* will get on, sharing the homespun wisdom and work ethic of the Waltons?

If you do decide you will help him out by providing accommodation, there are some important issues to address:

- ▶ **Tenure** – How long will this *temporary* arrangement last?
- ▶ **Rent** – How much will be paid towards household expenses?
- ▶ **Privacy** – Will there be 'private' rooms in addition to communal areas?
- ▶ **Visitors** – Will there be limits on numbers and rules regarding times and possibly days?

Perhaps most importantly, how will you ensure you all communicate problems before things get out of hand? Everyone should be encouraged to speak their mind rather than allowing things to fester. That said, your 'guests' should be under no illusion that they are anything more than that – short- or medium-term guests. The danger is that they will be incredibly grateful for a week or two but will then begin to accept the situation as the norm. If necessary, point out *once* that you, not they, are the owners of the property.

No room in the inn?
However if don't feel comfortable with anyone sharing your house, or if they're outstaying their welcome, tell them. Don't allow yourself to be the victim of any intentional or unintentional moral blackmail. Don't feel in any way guilty. Your prospective son-in-law and your daughter must understand that getting married is an adult life choice which involves taking on significant individual and collective responsibilities, including setting up their own household. In any case, they can always postpone the wedding, if they wish.

Try to turn what may well be perceived as a negative into a positive. Stress the benefits for them of living on their own. They will have all the privacy they want and need. They will be far more independent. And they will be making all their decisions, financial and otherwise.

He's from a different ethnic background
We live in a multi-cultural society and marriages between people from different backgrounds, races, religions and cultures are becoming more and more prevalent. For example, a recent survey revealed that 45% of British Asians would now consider marrying outside their race. Such a high percentage would have been unthinkable only a few years ago.

Whatever your feelings about the engagement, do not be judgmental and listen before you speak. Some people will argue that such a marriage will create unique problems, others will be far more positive: it will create unique opportunities.

Letting him in
Don't be pushy, but try to include him in some of your religious and cultural customs and traditions. Invite him to your church or synagogue. Show an interest in his temple or mosque and accept any invitation to visit it. Forge links and demonstrate to him that you want to become a part of his life – and you want him to become a part of yours.

When it comes to the practicalities of the ceremony, some compromise may be essential. Which traditions of each faith will be included and which will be excluded or modified? Or perhaps there will there be two ceremonies. Planned well, this wedding – and more importantly this marriage – has the potential to be a fantastic fusion of culture and tradition.

He's a she
The Civil Partnership Act 2004 came into force in 2005. This enables same sex couples to obtain legal recognition of their relationship. Although, legally speaking, they are not 'weddings' as such, civil partnership ceremonies pretty much follow the conventions of a civil wedding.

You will almost certainly know well in advance if your future son-in-law is actually to be your daughter-in-law. How you react to such a situation obviously is a very personal issue and is outside the compass of this book. However, as always, it is best to remember that your daughter is an adult and that, ultimately, it is your role to support her, not criticise.

BUT HE DIDN'T EVEN ASK ME

It is not unusual nowadays for a future son-in-law not to ask parental permission to marry their daughter. Don't take this as an affront. It almost certainly isn't. The world has moved on, and wedding etiquette is being dragged along behind it. Maybe he isn't even aware of the tradition of asking you for your daughter's hand. Or maybe he thinks this custom is inappropriate in the twenty-first century.

Perhaps it was your daughter's decision for him not to ask you. After all, she is not your property (or anyone else's, for that matter). It could be that she thinks it is courtesy enough to *tell* you rather than *ask* you. And she may have a point, especially if the two of you have not been that close over the years. Maybe she proposed to him, in which case perhaps *she* should be asking *his* parents.

Knowing the score

For some fathers and stepfathers, passing the torch presents few if any emotional difficulties. Typically they may not have been involved in much if any of the child-rearing and therefore have few, if any, memories of tap dancing lessons or plasters on grazed knees.

For others this can be a heartbreaking experience. If you do not approve of her choice of partner, ask yourself why you feel this way. Do you really think her fiancé is not the one for her? Or is the real reason that you are not comfortable with the whole situation?

The bottom line is that both he and your daughter are adults with inalienable human rights. To be blunt, if they both decide to get married, what right have you to stop them? If you do withhold your blessing, one of four things may happen:

▶ They will call off the engagement.
▶ They will postpone the wedding.
▶ They will continue with their plans to get married.
▶ They will still get married, but sooner than originally planned, possibly in a different location and without any family involvement.

Unless you can convince your daughter that her fiancé is a latter-day Jack the Ripper, it is highly unlikely that the engagement will be called-off. It is possible that they may agree on a postponement, especially if there is some financial incentive to do so. However, it is most likely that option 3 or 4 will prevail. So unless you want to drive your daughter away (metaphorically and possibly literally), ultimately you must respect their decision. And to do so with grace and humility.

Meeting the family

It's never easy to be the new kid on the block. Do you recall whether you were immediately welcomed into your wife's extended family with open arms? Or did the assimilation process take months, or even years?

While it may be tempting to try to fast track him into your family circle, it is far more preferable to allow things to develop at a slower, more natural pace. With the average length of engagements in Britain now running at almost 21 months, there should be plenty of time for him to get to know everyone before the Big Day.

Don't overwhelm him. Gradually and subtly get him more and more involved in everyday family tasks ('Could you collect a parcel from the sorting office?') and introduce him to other members of your family ('Any chance of dropping this off at Jane's on your way home?').

Getting to know you

Maybe you already know your future son-in-law well. It seems he's been around forever and he's become an honorary member of your clan, almost by default. On the other hand, perhaps you've only just met him and a little male bonding would not go amiss.

If you share a hobby or an interest, this could be the obvious ice-breaker. Otherwise let your relationship develop naturally over time. It is important not to put any pressure on him to do things or go places he may not wish to. Maybe he's quite a reserved character (and/or maybe you are). Make it clear that he is very welcome to join you, but also that there is no expectation on your part that he does so.

The important thing over the next few months is that you get to know him as a *person*, not just as your future son-in-law. To misquote Humphrey Bogart: 'Who knows, this could be the start of a beautiful friendship.'

PART 2

GETTING ORGANISED

What is Expected of You?

'There is a special place in heaven for the father who takes his daughter shopping.' (John Sinor)

So it's official – the decision has been made and the countdown has begun. The big question for you now is: What am I supposed to do? Well, traditionally the father of the bride had two major roles: to walk his daughter down the aisle and to have deep pockets.

Today, things are a little more complex and there are now as many sets of father of the bride duties as there are weddings. In other words, there are no longer any hard and fast rules and you will simply be expected to do what your daughter wants. She may want you involved big time; she may want you to be there to offer help and advice as and when required; or she may simply not require much if any assistance from you. Your best approach is to let her know that you'll always be there for her – and that you want to help and support her practically, emotionally and possibly financially, as best you can.

As we shall consider in the following chapter, your role may also be influenced by the structure of your daughter's family. Perhaps you are her stepdad, divorced from her mother or a single father. According to circumstances, your daughter may wish to divide traditional paternal wedding duties between you and another man who has been important in her life, or she may wish you to assume some additional duties traditionally associated with a bride's mother.

However your daughter decides to play it, you could well be asked to become fully or partially involved in many if not all of the following tasks during the build up to the Big Day.

MEETING THE GROOM'S FAMILY

Traditionally, the groom's parents would call upon the bride's parents shortly after the engagement was announced. This does not always happen today. However, it is advisable that you meet up – or at least communicate in some way – and earlier rather than later, especially if it is to be a short engagement. Clearly this process will become more complex if you are divorced and/or the groom's parents are divorced, especially if there are new partners on the scene. That said, it really is important that there is meaningful contact between all the 'main players'.

Hopefully, you will all get on well and, with the agreement of your daughter and son-in-law, you can soon be getting on with some serious wedding planning. You may even begin to develop a real friendship and perhaps meet them socially. That would be wonderful, on many levels. However, obviously this eventuality is far from certain and you should never 'push it', even if you believe you owe it to your daughter to do so.

Them and us?

You may feel you have absolutely nothing in common with these people. They are outgoing, you are reserved; they are townies, you are country folk; you are from diverse social backgrounds. But you are wrong. You *do* have something very important in common: your daughter and their son. Talk about *them*.

Even if you do not immediately hit it off, be aware that you will need to work together, for a while at least. After that you may only meet on the Big Day, at your daughter's home and at the occasional family get-together. So remain cordial. Who knows, they may not be as bad as you originally thought.

FUNDING THE WEDDING

The average cost of a wedding in Britain is now in the region of £21,000, although estimates do vary from survey to survey. In 2008, *Brides* magazine broke down the average costs throughout the UK (converted to descending order) as follows:

Item	Cost (£)
▶ Honeymoon	3,788
▶ Caterers	3,706
▶ Reception venue	3,450
▶ Engagement ring	1,913
▶ Wedding venue	1,653
▶ Wedding dress	1,180
▶ Photography/video	911
▶ Champagne/wine	771
▶ Wedding rings	602
▶ DJ/band	552
▶ Flowers	516
▶ Car hire	319
▶ Attendants' outfits	303
▶ Groom's gift	289
▶ Groom's outfit	272
▶ Cake	258
▶ Stationery	244
▶ Beauty	177
▶ Lingerie	101
▶ Headdress/veil	94

- ▶ Attendants' gifts   88
- ▶ Shoes   87
- ▶ **GRAND TOTAL**   <u>21,274</u>

Whether your daughter's wedding is going to cost more, less or about the same as this, at an early stage it is essential to agree precisely who will be contributing to the wedding pot and who will be paying for what.

Traditional weddings

In the past, the bride's father was expected to shoulder the majority of the wedding costs. Tradition dictated that he paid for:

- ▶ Engagement and wedding newspaper announcements.
- ▶ The dresses.
- ▶ Outfits for the father and mother of the bride.
- ▶ Flowers for the ceremony and reception.
- ▶ The photographer.
- ▶ Most of the transport.
- ▶ The wedding stationery.
- ▶ The reception and all its trimmings (the big one!).

The origins of this practice date back to a time when daughters were something you had to pay someone to take off your hands. Only thirty years ago it was still the norm for the bride's father to pay for almost everything. Today less than a fifth of couples rely entirely upon the bride's dad. The world has moved on and costs are now generally shared more equitably.

But what if you are expected to be one those traditionally generous fathers, but you simply can't afford it? If your funds won't stretch to paying for the whole wedding, don't start mortgaging your soul just to give your little girl the day she's dreaming of. Tell her what you can afford and be prepared to stick to it.

Modern weddings

With the average age of first time brides and grooms rising over the last thirty years from 23 and 25, to 29 and 31 respectively, more and more engaged couples are now financially independent and are tending to finance at least a significant proportion of their own wedding costs. Here are some of the most common ways in which twenty-first century weddings are funded:

► The bride and groom pay for the wedding themselves.
► The bride and groom may pay the majority of the costs with both families contributing towards elements that they'd like to help with, such as transport, the flowers or entertainment.
► The costs are divided equally between the two families.
► The two families offer to contribute a certain amount towards the wedding, to be spent as the bride (and groom) wish.
► If either or both sets of parents are divorced a compromise is found using a combination of options.

A recent survey suggests that some 64% of couples are now paying for everything themselves, with 31% relying on their parents (13% looking to both sets of parents and 18% being entirely dependent upon the bride's family). The remaining 5% are funding their weddings using a variety of other inventive methods.

Talk to your daughter and her partner to establish how they wish to go about funding their wedding. They may well offer to take responsibility for some of the wedding costs, and the groom's family may also be willing to chip in. If anyone but you is footing the bills for certain items, make sure you keep track of who is supposed to be paying for what. It is also important to keep copies of all invoices, so any subsequent queries about outgoings can be easily and amicably resolved.

Competitive Wedding Syndrome

The move from traditional quiet weddings to grand, glitzy, opulent affairs is being fuelled by lavish celebrity bashes splashed across the covers of *OK!* and *Hello* magazines. Posh and Becks sat on matching thrones in a gothic castle, while Jordan arrived at her wedding in a pink horse-drawn carriage and later partied along with Peter and guests on lobster and foie gras, served by opera singing waiters.

And where the so-called celebs go, fans follow, along red carpets strewn with rose petals. This is foolish fantasy. You cannot buy a dream wedding. Of course, it helps to have a *reasonable* budget. However, if your daughter wants her day to be magical and memorable, she needs to open up her personality, not her purse; to rely on her character, not on your cash.

Setting a budget

Once the total available spend has been established, the next big question to be answered is: Who will be responsible for budgeting and spending? Will contributors simply hand over set amounts to your daughter and allow her to spend them as she sees fit, or will they decide at the outset what they are going to pay for?

If your daughter has a good head for money, it is best for her to have the ultimate choice of how the money is spent. In this way, her fate is in her own hands and she has no-one to blame but herself for any overspending on such and such or any underspending on something else.

Helping her to prioritise

None of us have a bottomless pit of money. It is therefore important for your daughter to decide what is most important to her. An important 'economic law', known as the Pareto Principle, states that 80% of what is important is represented by 20% of what exists. For example, 80% of a country's wealth is likely to be held by 20% of its population and 80% of a company's profits may be generated by 20% of its customers.

In the case of wedding budgeting and expenditure, the Pareto Principle can usefully be re-named the Parento Principle. This law tells parents that 80% of what is most important to their daughter will be represented by 20% of what is going to happen on her Big Day. If you can help her identify this key 20% – perhaps for her it is to be the entertainment and the meal, or maybe it's the floral arrangements and the venue – then optimum use of financial resources may be achieved by targeting 80% of her overall budget towards this 20% of her budget sub-heads.

BEING HELPFUL AND SUPPORTIVE

Once again, your roles, duties and responsibilities will be dictated by your daughter's wishes. However, you should be forthcoming with offers of help (and know when to back off). Most brides-to-be would appreciate the following assistance.

Being there for her

Let her know that she can rely on you to provide emotional and practical support. Your role is to listen, to love and to provide a shoulder to cry on, 24/7. Remind her that the most important thing for the two of them is to make the wedding true to their personalities and not to try to please everyone else or to live up to other people's standards and expectations. Encourage them to do whatever makes *them* feel happy.

Be prepared to undertake both major and menial tasks. At times the most trivial of chores will assume mega importance: 'Oh no, who is going to blow up all those balloons?'

Keeping her calm

Another related role for a father of the bride is to act as a calming influence when things are getting on top of her. Reassure her that at times a little tension is inevitable. However, if she becomes really nasty, unpleasant or verbally abusive to you, just walk away. Never allow yourself to become her whipping boy. And don't be tempted to spend your way back into her good books. She probably already understands that 'money can't buy me love'. If she doesn't now, she will – someday.

Being a source of advice

Some people appreciate being given advice, others don't. You know your daughter's personality and temperament. Diplomatically step in when it's appropriate to offer a pearl or two of wisdom – but do butt out when it isn't. The advice you may proffer is not necessarily restricted to aspects of wedding planning. You may wish to pass on some thoughts about the institution of marriage or some legal and financial information that would be of particular value to an engaged or recently married couple. We'll return to this in Chapter 6.

Being flexible and understanding

Your daughter may have some tricky decisions to make. Who should sit at the top table (indeed should there even *be* a top table)? Who should walk her down the aisle? Who should make that speech? Try to understand her inevitable and unenviable difficulties and dilemmas and accept her ultimate decisions and compromises.

Keeping her mother in tow

Some mothers of the bride throw themselves into the planning process and may even try to take over. If this happens – and your daughter doesn't appreciate it – a good tactic is to liaise with your daughter to give her mum a single time-consuming task to keep her involved, yet only at the margins. If this ploy fails, tactfully explain to your wife that it's her daughter's Big Day and that she should only become involved in the planning to the extent that her daughter wants.

Liaising with the clergyman or registrar

You daughter and son-in-law should arrange a meeting with whoever is going to officiate. They may well appreciate your presence and input. While the officiator will do his or her best to accommodate their wishes, there may rules, regulations and restrictions they must comply with. Perhaps some traditional wedding music won't be sanctioned if the ceremony isn't in a church; perhaps there are places and times when photography or videoing isn't permitted; maybe confetti isn't allowed. Don't worry if it isn't. Bubbles make a wonderful substitute for confetti. Kids from 2 to 92 will have a ball blowing bubbles from those little plastic pots (perhaps covered with wedding wrapping paper) and the photographer is sure to capture some wonderful expressions on their faces.

Checking out suppliers

Do you have any areas of expertise that could prove to be of value during the planning and procurement process? A popular role is that of chief wine and champagne tester whose onerous responsibility is to sample and short-list the various beverages on offer (hopefully literally). Other potential assignments could include visiting reception sites, listening to musicians or DJs in action and comparing the styles of photographers and videographers.

Being a chauffeur

'So what's new?' I hear you ask. You may have donned the proverbial chauffeur's cap more times than you care to remember during her earlier years, but perhaps this practice has lapsed since she met her fiancé. During her engagement your daughter and wife may well appreciate lifts to potential wedding sites, florists, dress shops and the like. You could even go shopping with them, if you are all comfortable with the idea.

Your services may later be in demand to pick up guests from railway, bus stations or airports, to transport them to hotels and ferry them from ceremony to reception.

Helping to create the guest list

If you are not hosting the wedding, there isn't much you can do to influence the composition of the guest list, unless you are asked to make suggestions. However, if you are the official sponsor of the event, it seems reasonable for you at least to have your say. This is where things can become a little fraught, the dilemma being: while *you* may be paying, it is *their* wedding.

While some names on the list will probably be automatic choices, with a limited number of places available, a full and frank discussion may ensue as to who should be invited and who should not be. If you simply cannot agree, a possible compromise would be a four-way split. You and your wife, your daughter, her fiancé, and his parents each invite an equal number of guests.

But we **must** invite them!

Alternatively, your daughter could invite more people than originally anticipated. Mercenary, I know, but to keep within budget, the amount spent per head would then need to be reduced proportionately. After all, the cost of inviting 40 guests at £40 per head is the same as inviting 80 guests at £20 per head, or inviting 100 guests at £16 per head.

In practice, of course, if you switch roles from accountant to father for a moment, you will realise that every time you roll your eyes you are destroying a piece of your daughter's happiness. Ask yourself: Who should be placed higher in the pecking order, your daughter's friend or Aunty Vi, with whom your only contact is an exchange of Christmas cards?

Small can be beautiful

Each invitee should feel part of a privileged group, not a faceless label on a mail merge. If you have 100 guests, each one is a measurable percent of the dynamic. As numbers multiply, conga lines get unwieldy, and individual personality will be dispersed across the room rather than focused on the spotlight of energy around the bride and groom.

Often a big party separates into a series of smaller parties all happening in the same room. A limited guest list minimises anonymity, since no-one is relegated to the fiefdom of a table a mile from the main action.

Providing information for invited guests

Once the guest list has been finalised, you could offer to put 'invitation packs' together. Nowadays couples often send out far more than just the traditional invitation. A pack *could* include any or all of the following:

▶ The invitation (anything from PC-produced to personally designed or hand calligraphed).

▶ An RSVP card.

▶ Information about the sites of the ceremony and reception, such as their addresses, telephone numbers, email addresses and websites.

▶ A map showing locations of these venues.

▶ Information about parking (locations and charges).

▶ Details of facilities that are available (and perhaps are not available) for elderly and disabled people and families with young children.

▶ Any restrictions that apply, such as the prohibition of paper confetti, mobile phones or flash photography at specific times and locations.

▶ Information as to whether there will be a free bar (not recommended), a cash bar, or some other arrangement such as the provision to guests of drink vouchers or tokens. (This is a great idea since everyone gets the same value of free drinks and the bar budget will not have been exhausted by the time grandma asks for her first small sweet sherry.)

▶ A list of reasonably priced B&Bs and hotels.

▶ Details of local attractions for people who may wish to extend their stay into a mini break.

▶ Telephone numbers of local taxi firms.

▶ A form inviting guests to state any special dietary needs.

▶ A form inviting guests to select a recording to be played at the reception.

▶ A gift list (etiquette no longer requires guests to request this information from the bride's mother).

▶ A statement that the couple would appreciate a cheque or vouchers from a nominated store for guests to contribute as much as they wish financially towards one special gift, such as a home cinema system.

World Wide Wedding

You could even design – or arrange for someone else to create – a personalised wedding website. This is not an expensive option nowadays. Many of the major wedding information sites on the net now offer users facilities to put together their own pages of information which would include everything guests are likely to need to know – and probably a lot more.

Choosing a gift

Obviously the choice of gift(s) must be yours. However generous you may have already been with wedding costs and regardless of whether you have bought them a practical, material gift and possibly intend to help them out financially, you may wish to give the happy couple a more thoughtful and personal memento. The possibilities are endless. Here are just a few ideas:

► A framed photograph or watercolour of the ceremony or reception site.

► A unique vase, bowl or other artifact created especially for them by a local craftsperson.

► Anything personalised, such as champagne flutes.

The perfect wedding gift is usually the result of a little creativity, legwork or googling, not necessarily a high price.

Attending the rehearsal

A rehearsal of the ceremony is often held about a week before the real thing. While you would not be expected to arrange it, you would be expected to attend, along with the other principal members of the wedding party. This is an excellent opportunity to confirm that everything is in order and to reassure everyone (and to be reassured by them) that it'll be all right on the day. This would be a good time to invite the officiant to the reception. He or she may decline if they don't know the family well. However, at least you will have asked.

Family 4 Matters

'You can choose your friends, but you can't choose your family.'
(Proverb)

The traditional average family of mum, dad and 2.4 children no longer exists. Today families often come with a mum, dad, stepmum, stepdad, siblings, stepsiblings, and even step-stepsiblings. And at the same time, an ever increasing number of these families are scattering themselves all over the country – and often all over the world.

Given these sociological and demographic trends, weddings and wedding etiquette are necessarily changing. As families now come in such varied structures, more and more brides (and grooms) are wisely ignoring – or at least adapting – wedding etiquette, and relying instead on their common sense.

HAPPY FAMILIES?

A wedding is an occasion which brings people together. The problem, of course, is that not everyone gets on that well. Some people love each other, others like each other, others tolerate each other and yet others despise each other. The greater the number of people involved in the wedding celebrations, the bumpier the journey is likely to be. Your daughter knows this – and so do you.

The good news is there is no need to worry about what used to be considered to be 'proper' or 'correct'. Encourage your daughter to arrange things in a way that makes her feel most comfortable, perhaps by including or modifying some traditions and rituals that appeal to her and by disregarding others which she considers irrelevant or inappropriate. She may also wish to include something new that will drag the ceremony into the twenty-first century. That's fine, too. Who knows, maybe it'll catch on. Tradition has to start somewhere.

Rules of engagement

Don't assume the wedding will heal old wounds. That's a big ask. In fact, often the opposite can be the case with old arguments resurfacing. If things are not handled sensibly and sensitively, relations could easily deteriorate over the next few months – making the Middle East look like a picnic. At times you may feel the need to call in a UN peacekeeping force.

So how do you stop people fighting (possibly literally)? Try to establish some basic and civilised groundrules with which everyone can agree:

▶ No raised voices.
▶ No name calling.
▶ Everyone has the right to be heard.

Other than that, all you can do is retain your dignity and be seen to be impartial. Above all, remain calm. If you can keep your head when all about you are losing theirs...

DEALING WITH YOUR (FORMER) FAMILY

If there are family tensions or even feuds, your daughter will be placed in the unenviable position of trying to keep everybody happy. Unfortunately, this may not always be possible. At times, you may feel disappointed or even hurt by her choices. Difficult as this may sound, try not to take it personally or to feel slighted. She has some very delicate balancing acts to perform.

By all means talk to her and look for solutions if any arrangements are making you feel particularly uncomfortable. But don't embarrass her or make her life even more difficult by expecting any 'special treatment'. Empathise and support her – and ultimately respect her decisions. She will thank you for this.

Your ex

If you get on reasonably well, the fact you will both be present at the wedding and reception should cause no problems whatsoever. However, if your divorce was acrimonious and all you now have in common is your daughter, things could be tricky. How will your former wife – and possibly her new partner and stepchildren, together with your former in-laws – fit into the grand scheme of things? The answer must be: in precisely the ways your daughter wants them to.

Whatever your feelings toward your former wife, keep them to yourself. Don't say a single word against her. Smile graciously and be courteous, unchallenging and magnanimous.

I'm not going if **you** are

This is the nightmare scenario. Try to *communicate* with your ex, even if you haven't done so for years. Explain that your daughter shouldn't be forced to choose which of you to invite – and which one not to. Her day will not be as happy if you're both not there to share it with her. This is but one day in your lives, but it is the first day of the rest of hers.

I'm not going if you're bringing **her**

This is another extremely difficult situation. Once again, *talk* to your former wife. Is a compromise possible? Perhaps the new lady in your life could just attend the reception. However, be aware that if you simply cannot agree, your daughter may decide to exclude your new partner from everything, especially if the two of them do not get on.

How you react to this, of course, only you can decide. But do not give a knee jerk reaction. If you haven't done so already, think it through extremely carefully and discuss the options open to you with your partner. Remember that it's your daughter's day and this unfortunate situation is not of her making.

I'm not sitting next to **you**

We're on much safer ground here. Divorced parents do not have to sit together. If you really cannot stand each other, you can either both sit in the front row at the ceremony, but with other relatives between you, or you can sit in the row behind her. At the reception you can be seated at separate tables, each with your respective set of friends.

Mum's the word

As if your ex's very presence wasn't enough for you to bear, you may also face the double whammy of your daughter seemingly only being interested in *her*: 'Mummy said this...', 'Mummy did that...' Mummy, Mummy, Mummy! And isn't this the very same mummy who did the dirty on you all those years ago? How can your little girl be so gullible and insensitive?

The fact is that she is not trying to hurt you. However close you are to her, she wants her mother around at this important transitional stage in her life. The reasons for this may be both her emotional attachment to her mother and also the simple fact that she appreciates having someone around who seems genuinely interested in the design of her dress and the flavour of the cake. This is not a popularity contest between her parents. Try to understand what is going on in your daughter's head and don't react negatively to the situation. Mum's the word.

Your ex's new husband

The way you feel about her partner clearly will be influenced by the circumstances under which they got together. If he was the one who caused you to split up with your wife, it is hardly surprising if he is not at the top of your Christmas card list. However, if he met your ex several years after you amicably went your separate ways, your feelings toward him may be far more neutral. Either way, remember that your daughter should not be made to feel like piggy in the middle. She may well have found it difficult to cope with *your* divorce; don't make it difficult for her to cope with *her* wedding.

If the two of you get on reasonably well, or at least can co-exist without causing a scene, your daughter will be delighted. She may well ask you to share the traditional father of the bride duties with her stepfather. That would be an excellent compromise. However, if she wants her stepdad to act as the sole father of the bride, so be it. Remain dignified, charming and witty throughout and the guests will appreciate how well you will have handled and reacted to a tricky situation.

Your former in-laws

Once again, your relationship with your ex's family will largely be affected by possibly differing perceptions of what 'went wrong'. In their eyes, you may be may have been Mr Nasty; while to you it is obvious that you were (almost) blameless.

Whatever the cause(s) of the break up, it certainly was not your daughter's fault and, in any case, this is not the time for yet more recriminations. In an ideal world, of course, everyone would allow bygones to be bygones – for one day, at least. However, this is not an ideal world. Smile, nod and make small talk, if you feel able. But don't say anything contentious. And don't rise to the bait if anyone says anything contentious to you.

Your new wife

How well do the two most important women in your life get on? The fact that you love them both does *not* mean they necessarily love each other. If your daughter has 'taken sides', your new wife could either have pride of place, or could be horribly snubbed. Unless there have been issues such as physical, mental or sexual abuse, children usually want their parents to get back together and, as they see it, for happy families to be restored. Probably highly simplistically or even simply incorrectly, your daughter may have always seen your new partner as the only obstacle to the two of you doing just that.

You can't make your daughter love her new stepmum, or to even like her. However, unless your new partner has unquestionably and exclusively been responsible for some serious issues and problems that have directly or indirectly affected your daughter, it is not unreasonable to expect your daughter to at least *respect* your wife.

Your ex has vetoed her presence

As we have seen, your ex may have said she wouldn't attend if your new partner does. This presents a horrible dilemma for you. You could simply walk away. But if you do, then it may not be for just one day; you may be walking out of your daughter's life. It's a difficult call to make. Isn't it a pity how some separated parents do not realise that the only thing they now have in common is their daughter, and they are not willing to go some way to making up for the sorrow they caused her when they got divorced?

REMEMBERING THE CHILDREN

Children of all ages can be deeply affected by marriages and re-marriages. However complex or difficult your personal situation, do not say or do anything without firstly carefully considering how it may be perceived by *all* the children in your family network.

Your other children

While your attention is understandably focused upon your daughter, it is all too easy to ignore or neglect the feelings of your other children. What do they think about things, both individually and collectively? Siblings obviously can love each other, but they can also be highly jealous and envious of one another. When these emotions co-exist, as they may well do now, this can cause an emotional maelstrom.

It's not fair ...
A younger child may feel aggrieved that you appear to be treating her sister as an adult while you are always treating her as a child: 'She's only eighteen months older than me!' Does she have a point? Some fathers tend to see and treat their older children as mature adults and their younger ones as mere babies.

Perhaps one of your children has been living with a partner for some time. He hasn't received any financial help from you but now he sees you being incredibly generous to your prodigal daughter. Or maybe when he got married he had to pay most of the expenses himself because his wife's parents (and his) did not contribute. Why should his sister (and her fiancé) not have to make the same financial sacrifices as he did?

Money, money, money

Then again, maybe your financial situation has improved significantly since your first daughter got married. It had to be quite a modest affair. What must she be thinking now her sister seems to be being treated like royalty? Is she thinking you have done the best you could for both of them at the time, or is she resentful? 'He's always liked her more than me.'

Another potential dilemma can occur if one of your children has recently split up from a long-term partner and is feeling that her world has come to an end. How can you square the circle of appearing so happy for one daughter at the very time another is feeling so low?

Of course, there are ways to mollify if not totally satisfy disgruntled siblings. Perhaps a little cash or a gift might do the trick? Or maybe an understanding word is all that is required? That is up to you. The point is that you must remain aware that your daughter is not getting married in a vacuum.

Your step-children

It is possible that there may be long-running antagonism between your 'natural' children and your stepchildren. And if the wedding is to be quite a small affair, your daughter may wish to invite more friends at the expense of her stepsiblings. 'They wouldn't come, anyway', she argues.

However, if you want your stepchildren to be there (or at least to have been given the opportunity to be there), you should say so. Ultimately, money talks and, if you are paying you could insist. Yet it is far more preferable to convince your daughter that inviting her stepbrother(s) and/or stepsister(s) is the right thing to do. If she still wants to invite more friends, that's fine. She will simply have to cut back on some other area of the budget.

Their children

When one or both partners already have children, it is essential for the children's viewpoint to be taken fully into account. It is not always easy constructing a 'ready made' family and the more thoughtful and understanding your daughter and son-in-law can be in considering the happiness of the children, then the greater the chance of creating a warm and loving family for everyone. It is worth remembering that marriage is all about families and with a little thought this wedding could provide wondrous childhood memories for their children.

Once you are made aware of the engagement, tactfully advise the happy couple that the children should hear of the marriage from them and should be given time to get used to the idea before it is made public. Encourage them to listen to their children and to talk to them about the changes that will affect them when they have a new stepmother or stepfather.

You can help, too. Children can get some very strange ideas into their heads. One young boy thought moving in with a new stepdad meant leaving all the furniture and – far more importantly to him – all his toys behind in the old flat. Support your daughter by reinforcing her positive messages and by making sure the children understand and feel secure with the new arrangements.

Get them involved
The very idea of the wedding itself may be traumatic for the children of the bride or groom. It is their life that is changing as well as their parents', the difference being that the adults have chosen for themselves whereas the children are often just expected to fit in. Encourage your daughter to draw the children into the wedding plans. Make them feel they too have played a part in the decision-making process. And get them involved on the day itself.

▶ The wedding invitations could include the children's names, or even come solely from them.

▶ Separate invitations from the children could be sent to their own friends and young relatives.

▶ They could have their own miniature cake which they could ceremoniously cut at the same time their parents cut theirs. They would then be given the responsibility of handing it around to the younger guests.

▶ Alternatively or additionally, they could have their own 'reception'.

▶ Older children could be invited to take part in the ceremony by giving a reading, making a speech or proposing a toast.

▶ Sons and daughters could act as best man, ushers, bridesmaids or flower girls.

▶ The bride could be escorted down the aisle by her child or children, who could 'give her away'. (This option would also resolve your daughter's possible dilemma about 'which father' should do the honours.)

▶ A carefully chosen present from a new stepparent may be helpful. A little bribery can work wonders.

Children need to see that the marriage is being entered into enthusiastically by both partners and the fun of planning (yes, it can be fun!) can lead to a united family feeling before the great day arrives. When there are children involved, it should be a genuine 'family' wedding, not one just for the bride and groom.

Money Saving 5 Strategies

'A cynic is a person who knows the price of everything and the value of nothing.' (Oscar Wilde)

However large or small the overall budget, and regardless of who's paying for what, it's foolish not to always seek the best value for money. Whether you will be picking up the tab for the entire shindig, paying for some part of it, or have no financial commitment whatsoever, you are sure to find some useful tips and advice in this chapter which you can use or pass on to others.

Weddings are notoriously expensive. Average costs in the UK vary from survey to survey. However, an average of averages suggests the current outlay to be in the region of a gigantic £21,000 – a 100% increase over the last ten years. Yet there is a clear distinction between the cost of a wedding and the cost of a marriage. In England and Wales, you can marry at a register office for around £100. So how can you save on, or make better use of, that other £20,900?

Well, your daughter may be able to make some significant savings by shopping around for her wedding dress, getting her hair and make-up done on the cheap, having ready-made bouquets and sprays, and settling for a less lavish honeymoon. However, maybe you think all that's for her to decide. Similarly, if the guest list and the number of bridesmaids are cut down, so is the overall cost of the wedding. But these are also likely to be highly contentious issues.

This chapter is more concerned with providing more general money saving strategies and offering some specific tips on reducing 'non-personal' expenditure, such as the cost of the ceremony and reception, and the entertainment, photography, flowers and stationery. You and your daughter are unlikely to agree with all of them, but at least they will provide you with some valuable food for thought.

GENERAL ADVICE

The first thing to do is to agree a realistic budget with everyone who will be contributing financially. Then decide whether certain amounts should be allocated to various budget sub-heads – such as catering, transport and entertainment – or whether the bride (and groom) should be in control of the entire pot.

You will never underspend

In the same way that Parkinson's Law tells us that work expands to fill the time available, so Father of the Bride's Law, in short FoB's Law, tells us that wedding expenditure will expand to fill the funds available – and can often to exceed them. When was the last time you heard a newlywed ask: 'What are we going to do with the unspent cash?'? Therefore, be aware that, once disclosed, your established budget will be the *minimum* spend.

Neither a lender nor a borrower be?

When it comes to weddings at least, Polonius may have got this one wrong. Many people will say never borrow. True, we are living through a period of credit crunch where loans are far more difficult and expensive to obtain. However, whoever is funding the event they may decide it is so important to your daughter that they are willing to take out a loan. That's a personal choice. What undoubtedly would be foolish would be for anyone to get financially crippled as a result of the wedding. Any debts incurred should be carefully thought through and then tightly controlled.

Three key questions need to be addressed:

▶ Are the repayments affordable?
▶ Is the overall expenditure planned in such a way as to minimise the need for borrowing?
▶ Is the loan the best deal available?

It is never worth over borrowing. If you can't repay a loan, without undue discomfort and within a year, don't borrow it in the first place.

Employing a wedding co-ordinator?

The average UK bride spends 250 hours organising her wedding. That's equal to six full-time working weeks. If you and your daughter have hectic work schedules, or if she's getting married at a distance or just finds wedding planning too stressful, a wedding consultant could be the answer to everyone's prayers.

Wedding co-ordinators operate at a variety of levels and fees. Start-to-finish consultants handle absolutely every aspect of the wedding, but at a price. Others provide an array of services, which might be billed at an hourly rate or a fixed flat fee per service provided. This gives you the opportunity of choosing precisely where and when you need assistance.

A popular alternative is hiring a co-ordinator to manage events on the wedding day. The co-ordinator ensures everybody is in the right place at the right time, checks out the reception venue in advance to make sure everything is perfect, co-ordinates serving, pouring, toasting and cutting the cake and pays the bills, leaving you and your family to relax and enjoy the day. A cheaper 'just for the day' option could be to hire a professional toastmaster. He or she would fulfil similar roles, although they would probably not pay any bills on your behalf.

Hiring a wedding consultant might seem like an extravagant extra, but it could be the best investment you make. Their services can be secured for as little as £500, depending on the size of the wedding and your specific requirements. They can also often save you as much as this, if not more, by negotiating discounts with suppliers.

As always, personal recommendation counts for so much. It is essential to feel comfortable with the person you choose. When you meet prospective consultants, there are some key questions to ask yourself:

► Will this person push us into decisions we don't want or can't afford, or will they commit to our budget?

► Do they have a good rapport with the best suppliers (venues, caterers, photographers and so on)?

► Are they in a good position to negotiate discounts on our behalf?

► Will they be there on the wedding day, overseeing the entire event?

► Does this co-ordinator seem genuinely excited about the wedding?

▶ Would they be likely to make the right decisions and remain calm under pressure?

▶ Does the co-ordinator have insurance, both personal liability and professional indemnity?

A wedding consultant is a creative partner who should be able and willing to offer advice and opinions, in addition to looking after all the practical arrangements. They will help you prioritise, plan, consider risks and help you get the best value for money.

Visiting bridal shows and wedding fairs

This provides a great opportunity to see lots of different suppliers at one time rather than travelling to see different people around the country. While it may be rash to place orders on the day, you could ask them whether they would be willing to offer discounts if you were to order within a certain period following your visit.

Marrying abroad?

An estimated 30,000 British couples marry abroad every year. For these daring romantics, a wedding away is a quicker, easier and undoubtedly cheaper alternative to a big bash at home. They spend around £15,000 less than traditional, stay-at-home couples, forking out a more affordable £6,000 on a combined wedding and honeymoon.

You can find information on legal requirements for various destinations abroad at weddings.co.uk.

Be realistic

The wedding industry is based upon fantasy. Brides are bombarded with ideas to make their weddings more fun, more competitive –

and more expensive. With all this hype it's all too easy for even the most level headed person to get drawn in: that very same girl who was never the slightest bit interested in a donkey ride on the beach will now settle for nothing less than travelling like a princess in a horse-drawn carriage.

There is nothing wrong with wanting to create a unique and memorable event and, of course, a reasonable budget helps. However, the best way to achieve this end is to inject plenty of thought and personality, not plenty of cash.

Avoid the 'w' word

When you mention the word *wedding*, prices seem to get inflated by a factor of three or more. So keep negotiations as general as possible and only mention the 'w' word once a price has been agreed.

Rope in friends and relatives

Do you have a friend who is a DJ or a musician, an aunt who is an expert cake maker, an uncle who owns a vintage car? Try to make use of friends' and relatives' skills and possessions. Ask them for their help in lieu of a wedding present. Most people will be pleased to get involved.

Shop around and haggle

Start early. Shop round and compare notes. As a rule of thumb: always get at least three quotes. Don't be frightened to haggle (or get someone to do it for you, if you're not comfortable with that), after all, they will have haggled with *their* suppliers. If you have received a lower quote for the same product or service elsewhere, play them off against each other. At a regular auction, the *highest* bidder wins the spoils. This is a Dutch auction where, all things being equal, the *lowest* bidder gets your trade.

Be firm yet flexible

When you negotiate with potential vendors and service providers, be firm. Stick to what has been decided is required and don't allow them to talk you into anything you hadn't budgeted for. However, if nobody can provide precisely what you had hoped for you need to be flexible enough to negotiate a suitable alternative within your budget.

Read the small print

Be sure you are familiar with all changes, return and cancellation policies before you sign anything. Pay particular attention to deadlines for returning items. Keep copies of every contract and every receipt in a safe place.

Get googling

Search the internet thoroughly and you can save a lot of time and money. The World Wide Web provides information and resources for making purchases online. Many wedding websites provide links to wedding-related businesses that could be your answer to quality products and services at a reasonable price.

And don't forget good old eBay. It's a huge and very competitive marketplace. You may well find some great deals.

SPECIFIC ADVICE

There are loads of ways of reducing costs of a wedding, without reducing its quality. Only you know how your daughter is likely to react to the following ideas and suggestions. If you believe any of them 'have legs', why not tactfully discuss them with her? After all, if she makes savings in one area, there may be scope for additional expenditure elsewhere.

The ceremony

▶ Marry on a weekday. Many venues are much cheaper then than at weekends.

▶ Marry later in the day. The guests won't need to be fed twice.

▶ Get married on 1st April (April Fools Day) or on a Friday the 13th. Not many other couples will do this, so you could bag some real bargains.

▶ Avoid Christmas, Easter, Valentine's Day and Mother's Day. Because these times are so popular, costs hit the roof. Flowers, in particular, cost a fortune.

▶ If it is to be a civil ceremony, have the service and the reception at the same location. You may well get a discount for doing so and it would certainly cut down on travel costs.

The reception/wedding breakfast

▶ Hire an empty venue and bring in your own suppliers for real savings.

▶ If the numbers are not too daunting, do the catering yourself.

▶ Style the reception yourself. It can be time-consuming, but it is much cheaper. Inexpensive alternatives can be used instead of costly items, such as white bed sheets replacing tablecloths.

▶ At a sit down meal there needs to be adequate options for guests. However, the fewer the choices the lower the bill.

▶ One party is enough. A separate evening do is not necessary.

▶ Cooks and waiters can sometimes be hired cheaply from catering colleges.

▶ Remember that a buffet can often be cheaper than a sit down meal.

▶ Buy a ready iced but not decorated celebration cake from a supermarket or department store. These come in a variety of sizes, with pillars available to make tiers. Adding ribbon and figures on the top can create a personalised and affordable alternative to the traditional made to order wedding cake.

▶ Buy a sponge or fruit cake and then ice and decorate it yourself.

▶ Serve the cake as dessert. Consider lemon or chocolate instead of traditional fruit cake and ask the caterers to serve with fresh cream and berries.

▶ To reduce cost and waste, decorate and serve individual cup cakes.

▶ Avoid the cost of expensive wedding favours by making them yourself.

The drinks bill

▶ Use a bar. You can control how much you want to spend and when you've reached your limit, the guests then pay for themselves. Better still, to avoid a few beer monsters getting through all the money 'behind the bar' before anyone else gets a look in, give everyone the same value of drink coupons or vouchers.

▶ Go on a booze cruise and you could save a packet, though it's always worth checking this by pricing your booze list in the UK first and then using the internet to price it overseas.

▶ Find out about any corkage costs. There's no point in buying cheap booze, only to find that when the corkage is added it's no cheaper (or it's even more expensive) than the venue's own drinks.

► Try to negotiate your corkage or think creatively. If the corkage is a standard amount *per bottle*, it would be prudent to use the largest bottles you can find.

► Use a venue which allows you to bring your own drinks, yet does not have a drinks licence. This will mean even cheaper drinking, as there will be no corkage charges. To comply with the law, the reception must be a *private party* (this could be specified on invitations) and *no alcohol may be sold* during the event.

► Purchase your alcohol from a major store; they may offer a sale or return deal and a free glass hire service.

► Streamline with a signature drink. The wider the choice of drinks you serve, the higher your costs will be. Provide a cocktail or punch, or just offer wine and beer.

► Serve cava instead of champagne to greet the guests and for the toast.

Entertainment

► Make your own entertainment. Perhaps you could arrange a treasure hunt, or play some old favourites such as 'Pass the Parcel' or 'Musical Chairs' in the afternoon and play music via a CD player in the evening. Create a varied playlist to keep everyone happy and to avoid the cost of booking a DJ.

► Invite a talented amateur to act as your club DJ.

► If any of your guests are good singers or musicians, let them perform.

► Audition local college music students.

► Consider having a karaoke session (for a limited period).

Photographer/videographer

▶ Don't scrimp on the photographer. This is an area where it would be foolish to try to cut corners. Once the general style (posed, unposed or a combination of these) has been decided, consider precisely what is required and then compare the packages and prices of recommended professionals within your area.

▶ If you're not bothered about having snaps of you at the reception, book the photographer by the hour.

▶ Think carefully before allowing a family member or friend to undertake this pivotal role. They are unlikely to have the equipment or expertise of a professional photographer.

▶ Some couples opt for a camera club 'amateur'. This is also a high risk strategy as there are issues around liability insurance and insurance against equipment failure. Most amateurs are not covered.

▶ Many of the guests will be clicking away all day. Ask them for copies of their photos, videos and DVDs.

▶ Place disposable cameras on the tables at the reception and collect them in towards the end of the evening.

Flowers

▶ Buy flowers for decorating the ceremony from markets or greengrocers. They will be cheaper than those purchased from specialist outlets.

▶ Choose flowers that are in season. They cost more if they have to be flown in.

▶ Contact the other couples who are getting married at the

same place and on the same day, to discuss the possibility of sharing the cost of flowers.

► Transfer the flowers from the ceremony to the reception, where they can be placed on tables and at doorways.

► If the wedding is a day or two after a major religious event, it is likely that the church will still be lavishly decorated.

► Visit the British Heart Foundation. They sell cheap imitation roses which are ideal for button holes.

Stationery

► If the stationery is being printed, go for simple printing techniques. Anything glittery, embossed or engraved will be quite expensive. The simpler you go, the more you'll save.

► Find out if anyone's employer will allow them to claim a company discount on the stationery.

► Produce your own invitations. Be creative and make them personal and unique. It will save you a fortune. MadaboutCards.com has a great range of cards and card making accessories.

► When posting invitations, check the weight and size. To qualify for minimum postage they must weigh less than 100 grams and must be smaller than 240mm x 165mm x 5mm. Always send them second class. There's plenty of time, so two to three days for delivery is just fine.

► There is no need to supply stamped and addressed return envelopes for RSVPs. Give invitees the options of responding by email, phone or post.

► A *really* cheap option, if no-one minds an informal approach, is to email the invitations.

► When it comes to thank you cards, find a really nice photo of the newlyweds, have the negative reprinted as many times as necessary, and ask them to handwrite their personal words of thanks on the reverse of each.

So there we have it. When it comes to funding a wedding, having a reasonable budget obviously helps. However, there are also huge savings to be made if you are prepared to shop around and do a little homework. It's a question of getting the balance right – or rather, of getting *your* balance right. This is a massive day in your daughter's life and you certainly don't want to be remembered as the Scrooge who ruined it for her. But really it's the thought and personality that's put into a wedding – rather than the number and size of cheques thrown at it – that can make the event unique and memorable.

Offering Useful Advice

'I have found the best way to give advice to your children is to find out what they want to do and then advise them to do it.'
(US President Harry S. Truman)

As father of the bride, you may wish to pass on some words of wisdom, some exclusively to your daughter, and some to both her and her partner. Whether they wish to hear them, of course, is another matter. Only you will know if and when it is appropriate to make a few little suggestions.

Three areas of advice are discussed in this chapter: general, legal and financial. The general advice relates, in broad terms, to: 'What makes a happy and successful marriage?' We can only touch the surface here by pointing out apparently universal truths. You will have your own ideas, too. What makes *your* marriage work – or made it fail? Yes, we can learn from our failures as well as our successes. You have a wealth of life experiences to call upon and, as Oscar Wilde put it: 'Experience is what we call our mistakes.'

There follows some legal and financial information and advice likely to be of value to people who are about to marry or who have recently married. These sections are intended to be broad in nature. **An important disclaimer here: people should always take appropriate legal or financial advice before embarking on any course of action.**

GIVING GENERAL ADVICE

I would not presume to suggest that the following is anything more than a brief and sometimes personal view on 'the secrets of a happy marriage'. Anyone requiring more comprehensive discussion and debate should refer to the excellent specialist resources listed towards the end of this book.

Improving communication

Communication is about connecting with one another. To be able to communicate with honesty requires trust. Partners need to know that when they express their hopes and fears, they will be listened to and their innermost thoughts valued, not met with rejection or ridicule. When someone really listens to you and gives you their undivided attention, you feel valued, special – and loved.

Recognising and respecting their differences

Everyone is different. The way your daughter's family and your son-in-law's family communicated as they were growing up will have had a significant impact upon the way they communicate as adults. One may have come from a family where feelings were never openly acknowledged or discussed. The other's family may have been loud and gregarious, with everyone and everything brought out into the open. Similarly, their individual personalities, whether they are natural extroverts or introverts, logical or intuitive, will have a telling effect on how they communicate.

The important thing is that each recognises the uniqueness of the other and does not expect them to become a clone of themself. Over time each will make adjustments in the ways they interact, largely without realising they are doing so. At this stage, if they do not already, they need to understand their different attitudes and preferences.

This is a useful exercise to help establish or confirm your daughter's and son-in-law's domestic priorities. Where would each of them place themselves on the following continuums?

Clothes	Casual	Formal
Disagreements	Thrash it out	Keep the peace
Holidays	Adventurous	Restful
Money	Spend	Save
People	Spend time with others	Spend time alone
Planning	Make plans	Go with the flow
Punctuality	Have time in hand	Cut it fine
Relaxation	Go out	Stay at home
Sleeping	Go to bed late	Get up early
Sport	Enthusiast	Uninterested
Telephone	Talk at length	Keep it brief
Tidiness	Immaculate	A mess
Television	Keep it on	Throw it out

(Source: adapted from *The Marriage Course Manual* [Alpha International Publications].)

Where there are big gaps, compromise may be necessary. But each partner has to feel that it's reciprocal. One can't feel that they're making all the compromises. When one spouse makes all the compromises, it's uncomfortable for both – not just the one giving in.

Honesty is the only policy

It is essential that they are truthful in their communication and they learn to talk together about how they feel. They need to know they can depend upon one another while retaining their independence. This includes resolving to have no secrets and to share their thoughts and feelings, their hopes and dreams. They need to allow each other to develop and grow at their own pace.

It's not (just) what they say, it's the way that they say it
Remember that 35% of our communication is tone of voice; 55% is body language. If a person says, 'What's the matter now?' with hands on hips and the emphasis on *now,* they will be conveying an entirely different message than if they spoke those very same words in a gentle tone with a sympathetic hand on their partner's shoulder.

Being positively positive

A happy and successful marriage is about knowing your partner, being supportive and being a pleasant person. Research shows that for every one negative thing a person does, in order to maintain the status quo, they need to do five positive things. When either partner makes a criticism, shows anger or becomes disrespectful, they need to counter-balance this negativity in five constructive ways, such as:

- ▶ Expressing their love.
- ▶ Showing appreciation.
- ▶ Giving greater attention.
- ▶ Giving a little surprise.
- ▶ Being nice.

But, of course, they shouldn't only do positive things after having said or done something unpleasant. They need to continually make small loving gestures. Little things matter. While it sounds easy, this commitment to being nice is no small matter. Most of the time it merely requires a little thought and consideration.

However, it's a lot harder to be nice when the pressure is on, when one or both partners is really angry, or when something perceived as unacceptable has happened for the umpteenth time. Nevertheless, for the relationship to work the overall balance must be heavily, heavily stacked on the positive.

Happily married couples aren't smarter, richer, or more psychologically astute than others. But in their day-to-day lives, they have hit upon a dynamic that keeps their negative thoughts and feelings about each other (which all couples have, to some degree) from overwhelming their positive ones. They have developed what can be described as an emotionally intelligent marriage.

In the words of that old Bing Crosby number:

> 'You've got to accentuate the positive
> Eliminate the negative
> And latch on to the affirmative
> Don't mess with Mister In-Between
>
> You've got to spread joy up to the maximum
> Bring gloom down to the minimum
> Have faith or pandemonium's
> Liable to walk upon the scene.'

Handling conflicts

Conflicts are inevitable in any relationship. In reality, some marital disputes don't ever get fully resolved. There will always be issues around in-laws, priorities, children. Solving the problems doesn't really matter. What's crucial is keeping things positive. You have to accept the other person's perspective and have an appropriate discussion without getting critical or blaming.

Couples who have good marriages retain their mutual respect and understanding of each other – even during discussions of their differences. They understand that in order to keep things positive, often under difficult circumstances, both of them must:

▶ Learn to communicate ideas and feelings.
▶ Choose an appropriate time and place to talk.
▶ Stay calm; if necessary, by asking for a short 'time out'.
▶ Learn not to 'win' an argument.
▶ Consider their partner's point of view.
▶ Not be hostile or go on the defensive.
▶ Not retreat into silence.
▶ Learn how you are different.
▶ Bring things up in a non-threatening way.
▶ Use *I* statements, not *you* statements. ('I'm concerned about our finances...'; *not*, 'You're wasting our money').
▶ Discuss issues, not personality qualities.
▶ Not use a current argument to bring past arguments back to life.
▶ Resist the temptation to say, 'While we're about it, another thing is...' (it is extremely difficult to resolve multiple issues at the same time).
▶ Learn to say sorry.
▶ Forgive and leave behind.

Couples must also stay in touch with their special ways of repairing the relationship. It can be humour, an early night, or whatever helps diffuse the situation. In happy marriages, over time couples learn to do this naturally. They deflect the anger, and get back on an even keel.

GIVING LEGAL ADVICE

Marriage is a contract with specific legal requirements which arise from that contract and affect the rights and duties of the parties and their legal relationship with third parties, including any children they may have. It is important that your daughter and son-in-law understand this, are aware of the legal formalities involved in getting married and are cognisant of other existing legislation which potentially may be relevant to them.

Please note that the following advice and information are provided for general guidance and are not a complete statement of the law. For further information on any aspect of the formalities to, or the ceremony of marriage please seek the advice of the superintendent registrar at the local register office. More generally, people should always take legal advice before embarking on any course of action.

The engagement

Since 1970 engagement has not been a legally binding contract so parties cannot sue for damages if it is broken off. There is usually no legal duty to return the ring.

Pre-nuptial agreements

While traditional wedding vows might contain a commitment to stay together until death, the statistics prove this does not always happen. If your daughter is marrying later in life, or for a second or subsequent time, and she is worried about protecting her assets, it may be worth considering setting up a pre-nuptial agreement (pre-nup).

A pre-nup is a written contract entered into by two parties who are about to marry with the intention of setting out their respective financial intentions and obligations in the event of a subsequent divorce. Although pre-nups are not legally binding under English law, if one exists its contents will be considered in divorce proceedings. Raising this matter while deciding on the guest list and honeymoon destination is far from romantic but, realistically, it *could* save a lot of hassle – and money – some time in the future.

Legal formalities for getting married in England and Wales

Under the Marriage Act, 1994, which came into effect the following year, a marriage may be held in a place of religious worship, a register office or public premises officially registered for marriages by the Registrar General for England and Wales. Civil marriages may now therefore occur in *seemly and dignified venues*, such as stately homes, civic buildings or hotels (but not open-air venues) which have been officially registered for the purpose.

Whether they get married by a religious ceremony or civil ceremony, the following legal requirements must be met:

▶ The marriage must be conducted by a person or in the presence of a person authorised to register marriages in the district.

▶ The marriage must be entered in the marriage register and signed by both parties, two witnesses, the person who conducted the ceremony and, if that person is not authorised to register marriages, the person who is registering the marriage.

Scotland

In Scotland, because it is the minister, priest, celebrant or clergyman who carries a licence, in theory, a religious ceremony can be performed almost anywhere, either in- or out-of-doors. It should be mentioned though that different churches and individual clergymen may have their own views on:

▶ marrying couples who are from outside their parish
▶ performing wedding ceremonies in locations other than in their church.

Couples should contact the minister concerned to ensure that he or she would be willing to carry out the ceremony should either of the above points be relevant.

Northern Island
There is less choice about where couples may marry in Northern Ireland, as it was excluded from the Marriage Act 1994 which allowed venues authorised by the local authority to be used for weddings.

Legal documents required before the wedding ceremony
▶ The couple will need to show documentary evidence of their names, ages and nationalities – ideally in the form of their passports.

▶ If they are under the age of 18, they will be required to bring a completed parental consent form.

▶ They will also be asked to provide evidence of their addresses.

▶ If either has recently changed their name, they may be required to bring their original birth certificate and the Statutory Declaration of Name Change certificate.

▶ If they are getting married in church, they will be asked for all documents relating to their banns.

▶ If either has been married or registered in a civil partnership before, they will also need to produce documents that confirm that they are now free to marry. These could be a divorce decree absolute or final order of civil partnership dissolution bearing the court's original stamp – or the death certificate of a former husband, wife or civil partner. If they have been married more than once before, only the paperwork relating to the most recent marriage is required.

▶ If they are subject to immigration control, they will also need to produce documentary evidence to confirm that they satisfy the eligibility requirements and to show that they have written permission by the Secretary of State to marry within the UK.

Are there specific days when couples aren't allowed to wed?
Legally, civil wedding ceremonies can take place between 8am – 6pm on any day, excluding Christmas, Boxing and New Year's Day. However, registrars in different county council boroughs will have different rules and regulations of their own, so your daughter would be wise to contact her local register office to double check.

Getting married abroad
If couples wish to marry abroad according to the laws of that country, then they will need to find out about the regulations that apply. To marry in another country often involves a minimum period of residency. Most countries will require couples to produce some kind of documentary evidence. To find out the requirements they should contact one of the following:

➤ the relevant embassy or high commission in this country

➤ the relevant register office where they wish to have their wedding

➤ the Marriage Abroad Section at the Foreign and Commonwealth Office in London (Tel: 020 7270 1500).

If they are informed that certificates of no impediment are required then they will need to contact the Register Office in whose district they reside to arrange to give notice of their intention to marry.

While the vast majority of marriages that take place abroad are recognised as valid in this country, they cannot be registered in the United Kingdom. In certain circumstances, however, it may be possible for the certificate issued by the overseas marriage authority to be lodged with the General Register Office. This would enable them to issue a certified copy of the document at some time in the future, if required. Further advice can be obtained from the General Register Office (Tel: 0151 471 4801).

Same-sex 'marriages'
Same-sex couples are now able to enter into a civil partnership by registering a formal commitment to one another. This gives them legal recognition for their relationship, which means they have almost exactly the same rights and responsibilities as married couples.

Legally, does your daughter have to change her name?
No. There is no official requirement for a woman to change her surname, but if she wants to take her husband's name, she is legally entitled to do so. Using the same surname as her husband is traditionally the easiest option for women, especially when children

are involved. For this, she would need to inform the appropriate government departments, banks, and other such organisations after her marriage.

Alternatively, her husband could change his surname to hers, by deed poll. A modern alternative is to make the new surname double-barrelled. Again for this, they would both need to arrange for this to be done by deed poll. Established businesswomen tend to prefer to keep their existing names, using the title Ms. Your daughter could keep her original surname for work, and use her husband's surname for personal life. Really, she has the freedom to decide which is most appropriate for herself and her husband.

Whom does she need to inform of her change of name?

If she does decide to go with the tried and trusted procedure of taking on her husband's surname then although she does not need to go through deed poll, she will need to notify a lot of people and organisations, supplying proof of marriage in most cases. Most of these establishments will need to be notified in writing. It is a good idea to write a standard letter informing people of her change of address. This can be saved on her PC and the relevant address and reference number for each organisation can then be added to this template.

Government departments, banks and building societies will need to see the original document or a certified copy to make the changes, but most other establishments will simply need a photocopy of the marriage certificate. Your daughter needs to think about each and every aspect of her life so that her name is changed on all the appropriate records and documents. This is a typical checklist of whom she should notify:

- bank
- building society (mortgage and/or savings accounts)
- clubs and societies
- college/university
- credit card and store cards
- dentist
- Department of Health & Social Security
- doctor
- Driver and Vehicle Licensing Agency
- employer
- finance/loan companies
- Inland Revenue
- institutes such as universities, etc.
- insurance companies
- internet service provider
- investment companies, including premium bonds and shares
- land registry
- local authority (council tax and register of electors)
- mail order catalogue companies
- mobile phone company
- motoring organisations
- optician
- Passport Office
- pension company
- professional institutes and bodies
- telephone company
- TV Licensing Office
- utility companies (water, sewage, electricity, gas).

Her new passport
If she wishes, your daughter may change the details on her passport

before she gets married, so she could leave the country on her honeymoon with her new name. She would need to pick up a form from a post office at least three months in advance and send it back to the Passport Agency.

Her new passport will be post dated and will not be valid until after the wedding. If she intends to travel abroad during the engagement period, it would therefore be better to retain her old passport and to purchase tickets in her current name. After the wedding, she would be required to obtain a new passport but would be permitted to use her old one for a short time under her new name.

FINANCIAL ADVICE

Getting married is an exciting and meaningful stage in any relationship. But often, in all the excitement and planning, money and financial issues can get lost, buried or simply ignored. Managing money in a partnership is critically important and careful control of it will help both partners navigate through many situations and potential problems.

Brides-to-be would often rather give themselves a beauty makeover than a financial one. But couples need their heads firmly screwed on and should take a long, hard look at their finances as they enter marriage.

The advice and information which follows are intended to be of a general nature. People should consult a professional advisor regarding their finances and any changes they may wish to make. There may well be tax implications to consider before they take any action – and legislation referred to below may change.

Saving for the wedding

Unless they are planning a very long engagement, most analysts agree that instant access savings accounts are the best place for the wedding fund. This is because, with plenty of bills to settle during the build up to the Big Day, they'll need to be sure funds are available when they need them. There's plenty of choice among the savings accounts, both on the high street and the internet. The competitive market conditions ensure that, if they shop around, they can get a reasonable interest rate.

As their savings are short term, they might consider taking advantage of an account which attracts a bonus. These are commonly available for anything from three months to a year and can bump up the interest rate by as much as a further percentage point. However, they should also ensure they don't inadvertently leave their savings in such an account after the bonus is paid. Once the bonus is removed, these accounts have fairly pedestrian interest rates so it would be wise to switch to somewhere offering a better rate.

Whichever savings account, or accounts, they go for, they should watch out for any conditions. Some accounts stipulate the number of withdrawals that can be made, the amount of money they have to pay in, or the length of time they have to retain the account. Interest may be lost if these rules are not followed.

Assuming they haven't already used up their ISA allowances, mini cash ISAs are also a great way of saving because interest is paid tax-free. And, because rates are usually a little higher than standard savings accounts, they're worth considering even if they are not taxpayers.

Financial tips for newlyweds

After the wedding bells stop ringing and bills cascade through the letterbox, many newlyweds find their physical and emotional compatibility can be compromised by their financial incompatibility.

Money is a major sticking point in many new marriages and the number one cause of divorce and marital disputes. Communicating about money is one of the top challenges for even the most open and articulate couples. But open communication is just the beginning. Financial experts Sam Goller and Deborah Shouse offer the following ten tips which you can pass on to the newlyweds:

▶ **Be honest with each other before (and after) tying the knot.** Avoid a fight about money after the honeymoon by talking about your individual financial situations before the ceremony.

▶ **Spend time talking about money memories.** Most people underestimate the impact their upbringing and traditional roles have on their current financial decisions. Sharing the past can relieve tension in the future.

▶ **Know when to pursue a money conversation, and when not to.** People who are tired, hungry or involved in cooking dinner aren't in a good frame of mind for holding meaningful money conversations. You should talk about such issues at a time when you're both calm and rested.

▶ **Get your priorities right.** Prior to formulating a financial plan, talk about what really matters to each of you when it comes to money.

▶ **Find out where the money's going.** Before you can spend your money in a way that gives you the greatest pleasure and helps you meet your goals, you have to understand your spending habits. Consider keeping a spending journal to find out where your money really goes.

▶ **Eliminate credit card debt.** Newlyweds can't afford to fall deeper into debt than they already may be. Make paying off credit card debt a top priority.

▶ **Create an emergency fund.** What if a financial emergency strikes? Three steps to get you started on an emergency fund are:
1. Determine how much you need.
2. Decide the best way to save consistently.
3. Find a safe place to put your savings.

▶ **Find a system that works for you.** Maybe it's sitting down together each month to pay the bills as a team. Or maybe one of you is better at handling expenses than the other and prefers to do it alone. Find a system that works for you both.

▶ **Don't stop talking.** To enjoy continued financial success as a couple, it is necessary to continue your money conversations on a regular basis. Many experts recommend sitting down with your spouse monthly to make sure you're still on track.

▶ **Appreciate that spending doesn't always have to be about money.** One of marriage's greatest rewards is spending time together. Learning and expanding your horizons as a couple or with friends can offer greater returns than any purchase.

(Source: adapted from *Yes, You Can Achieve Financial Harmony: A newlyweds' guide to understanding money*, Sam Goller and Deborah Shouse.)

As Goller puts it: 'Achieving financial success doesn't have to be stressful, but it requires determination. Newlyweds have a huge advantage when it comes to investing for the future – *time*. By taking the time now to build a solid financial foundation, attaining financial independence is a real possibility.'

Coping with combined finances

When people get married there are so many things they have to begin thinking about in the plural rather than the singular. Money is a key issue in this category. Here are some suggestions that should help:

► Opening a joint account, in addition to retaining their own separate accounts, is an excellent way of dealing with combined finances.

► Some couples deposit the same amount each month, others base their contributions upon an agreed percentage of their earnings.

► This account can be used to pay for joint expenditure, such as food, utility bills, holidays, insurance, mortgage/rent and household repairs/home furnishings.

► One of the greatest causes of unrest is the use of a joint account for personal expenditure. If one of them has a passion for Harrods while the other prefers Oxfam, it would be sensible for each of them to use their own current accounts for 'non-joint' expenditure such as clothes, hobbies and all 'frivolous' purchases.

► The concept of 'what's mine is yours, what's yours is mine' is fine, in theory. However, it would still be sensible to keep proper records of all outgoings.

▶ If things do go horribly wrong, then a joint account is designed to protect both partners. If either one blocks it, then the other will not have access to it either. The account will then remain blocked until the bank is informed of how they would like the account to function in the future.

Ensuring financial security

People getting married may wish to take out one or more financial products to ensure financial stability if something unpleasant happens to either of them. It is essential that they seek independent professional advice concerning the following, according to their personal circumstances:

▶ Writing (new) wills.
▶ Ensuring adequate pension funding for retirement.
▶ Arranging or reviewing insurance/assurance policies.
▶ Reviewing mortgage and other loan protection insurances.
▶ Advising employers' pension scheme administrators of a spouse as the death-in-service nominee.
▶ Considering optimum tax efficient savings products.

Buying a house together

Getting married is a life changing step that very often goes hand in hand with buying a house. With the commitment of marriage comes a degree of permanency and looking to the future, so thinking about where to live becomes a consideration involving decisions about the appropriate environment in which to bring up your children, as well as long-term financial planning. Bearing all this in mind, couples need to equip themselves with as much financial knowledge as possible so that when they make their mortgage decision they can rest assured that it is the best option open to them.

Getting that mortgage

If a mortgage will be required, it's very useful to obtain a 'mortgage in principle' *before* they even start looking for a house to give them the edge over any competition. This is a conditional offer made by a mortgage lender that they will, in principle, give the loan discussed. Having one of these means they should be able get the actual mortgage more quickly when the race to buy their chosen home begins.

There are literally thousands of different products available on the market. Each type has potential advantages – and disadvantages, depending upon a particular couple's circumstances and the current and future state of the economy. They should seek *independent* specialist advice before choosing a mortgage provider.

The deed is done

Solicitors should ask house purchasers how they want the deeds to be worded. This question merits serious consideration by both parties when purchasing a property jointly as man and wife.

Property in England and Wales may be owned in an individual's **sole name** (for example, that of the husband or wife), or as **joint tenants**, or as **tenants in common**. Different rules apply in Scotland and elsewhere.

If two people own a house as joint tenants, then, when one of them dies, the other person will automatically become owner of the whole house (regardless of the terms of the deceased owner's will). If, on the other hand, two people own their home as tenants in common, each person only owns a share in the home (usually quantified according to their contribution to the purchase price). When one tenant in common dies, his or her share will pass into their estate and be dealt with by their personal representatives, either under the terms of his or her will or according to the so-called rules of intestacy. Therefore a tenant in common can leave their share in their will, unlike a joint tenant.

Most married couples opt for the joint tenancy option. However, if your daughter already has children from a previous marriage and wishes to leave at least some of her property assets to them, or if she has paid more than 50% of the cost of the property, she needs to consider the tenants in common option.

A final financial word

Marriage is good for you! According to Andrew Oswald, Professor of Economics at Warwick University, getting married results in improved health, with a married person having a 9% lower risk of dying over a seven year period compared with an unmarried one. There are also financial benefits to tying the knot, with married people earning between 10% and 20% more than their single colleagues. Equally importantly, according to the good professor, marriage brings the same amount of happiness as an income of £70,000 a year.

Preparing **7**Your Speech

'To create a memorable speech requires excitement, empathy, warmth, enthusiasm and flair. Flair is the sizzle in the sausage.'
(Bob Monkhouse)

Think of your speech as a gourmet meal. Your opening lines should serve up a tasty starter that really whets the audience's appetite for the main course. Your closing lines should provide a delectable and memorable dessert with a delicious aftertaste.

Your aim is to create an awe inspiring and entertaining speech that will be remembered for years to come, and for the right reasons. Not much to ask? Well, no it isn't, if you follow the advice, tips and guidelines that follow.

GETTING THE TONE RIGHT

Great speeches come from the heart. Every father is different; every father-daughter relationship is different; every extended family dynamic is different. Precisely what you say, and how you say, it will be affected by these and other factors. However, regardless of your personal circumstances and the degree of formality of the wedding, it is undeniably true that this is an extremely important day in your daughter's life and your speech should reflect this. It should be:

► **Emotional**
  Don't stifle emotion. You should feel free to display strong

personal feelings. Describe an incident or two that demonstrates the joy you and your wife have had bringing up your daughter and the pleasure you have found in getting to know your new son-in-law – and his family. However, you must be genuine. False heartiness, cheap sincerity and – worst of all – crocodile tears will be all too obvious to an audience.

▶ **Optimistic**
This is not the time to share your personal woes, paint a gloomy picture of the present or offer dire predictions about the future. Stress your certainty that in her husband's care, your daughter will prosper along with him and – with a little homily on the 'give and take' necessary to a successful marriage – the confidence you have that happiness must accompany the love they so evidently bear for one another.

▶ **A tribute to the happy couple**
Refer to some positive characteristics of both the bride and groom that are *well known* to the audience (perhaps speak of your 'devoted daughter' and her 'hard-working husband'). Then declare your confidence that they will make all the effort needed and will not be found wanting. This is a marriage made in heaven. They were made for each other.

This above all: To thine own self be true

Don't buy a speech. It cannot be original, personal and relevant, no matter what 'personalisation' sites might tell you. If you accept the role, you shouldn't treat your speech as a chore where you look for an easy way out.

Many people have donated their speeches to wedding websites. Highly laudable, I'm sure, but they are of little value to a thinking father of the bride. If you crib jokes and one-liners from 5-star speeches, the odds are that many in the crowd will have heard them delivered by other speakers who have cherry-picked exactly the same material. This will immediately undermine your entire speech.

What possible value can there be in relating someone else's sentimental reminiscence in your speech? None. Everything you say needs to be thoughtful and unique, a loving reminder that our imperfections are part of our charm, and the sentiments of love, family and friendship shared together on this day are the truly important wedding accessories.

CONVEYING EMOTION

What can make your speech gripping is its potential to *involve* the audience on a subjective level, to make them empathise with your deepest feelings, to forge a bond between them and you.

It's all well and good *saying* how much you care for your daughter, how confident you are that she has made the perfect choice of husband and how sure you are that they will have a wonderful future life together. The audience may well think, 'How nice', but they won't be moved.

Far too many fathers make the mistake of dwelling on their own feelings and reactions and can be stunned to discover that no-one else in the room can relate to their genuine sentiments. 'But I was almost in tears as I was saying this,' they protest. 'How could the guests not be similarly moved?' How indeed?

Emotions are abstract concepts

The problem is that our feelings are *abstract*. It is not that we do not hear or understand abstractions, but without a visual peg, without something we can conjure in our minds with colour and form, intangible ideas and concepts that make little impact are soon forgotten.

Two other factors are involved here, and neither has anything to do with the hardheartedness of the guests. Firstly, when we try to describe the physical symptoms associated with a particular emotion – be it sadness, happiness or delight – there is little room for surprise, for creating a wow factor. We all know how it feels first hand.

The paradox is that in order to hold an audience's attention, we need to provide some new or profound angle, spin or insight into these emotions. Yet how can we say something different and meaningful about universal feelings?

Secondly, no matter how original your description of your emotions, it does not alter the fact that that those emotions belong to *you*, not to *your audience.*

Talk about the incident, not the emotion

So what is the solution? The best way to convey your feelings is to focus upon an incident which illustrates them. Concentrate, not upon the emotion that was evoked, but on the situation which gave rise to it. Turn abstract ideas into strong, concrete mental images. What you must do is to take each guest by the hand and guide them through your valley of emotions without ever having to mention any of those emotions by name.

Don't bore the audience with long introductions or unnecessary explanations. Get straight to the heart of the matter. Focus on a single incident or situation; provide a snapshot and it will keep the image alive in their minds and hearts. The more apparently mundane and ordinary the circumstances surrounding the occasion, the more powerful and extraordinary will be the emotion it evokes.

> *Having never married before and with no children of my own, I wasn't sure what my role as 'father' was. I talked to lots of people who all gave me contradictory advice. I read some books, which made me even more confused. I really had no idea what to be to (daughter). Luckily, I didn't have to – she made the decision for me. Something wonderful happened. Without any encouragement from me or (wife), one day she called me 'Dad'. Such a simple word, but one so unfamiliar to me. It was wonderful and I thank you eternally for saying it.*

People want more than to listen to stories, however well they may be told. They also want to experience one or two good, soul-satisfying, lingering emotions. Think about your favourite books, music, films. Don't they all share this lingering quality? Your aim is to create a mental image that packs a real emotional punch, to use words and images that elicit just the right response.

Less really is more

As father of the bride, you are expected to indulge in a little emotional outpouring as you say how much you care for your daughter, declare your confidence that she has made the right choice of husband and include a few positive thoughts about love and marriage in general. The problem is that an unremitting, relentless stream of gushing, florid language can come across as pretentious and insincere.

The simple, yet highly effective solution to this apparent dilemma is to use sincerity and emotion with caution and restraint, to spread them thinly throughout your speech, like caviar, and not pile them on thickly, like marmalade.

Memories allow us to smell roses in December.

I am her father, but she is my hero.

One or two well-chosen, genuine expressions of your strong personal feelings will be far more effective and memorable than a whole series of half-hearted passing references to the pleasure and delight you are experiencing on this most happy of days.

Choosing the right stories
This is a day charged with emotional intensity. Be passionate. Passion is contagious.

You need to open your heart and display your feelings through the stories you relate. Ask yourself: Do I really want the guests to know every last detail of my daughter's Saturday morning tap-dancing lessons, or do I want to share something deeply meaningful and joyous in our otherwise crazy world? Well, which would you prefer to hear?

As the writer C.S. Forrester reminds us, 'There is no denying the fact that words spoken from the full heart carry more weight than all the artifices of rhetoric'. It has been said that life is made up of moments, maybe a dozen or so times when something happens that literally changes your life. Can you recall a moment that revealed something significant about your daughter's personality or maybe one that had a profound effect on your relationship with her?

The great thing about a story is that you dream it as you tell it, hoping that others might be drawn along with you, and in this way memory and imagination and language combine to create spirits in the mind. The challenge is always to find that one story or anecdote that will portray all you want to portray.

> *(Daughter) had climbed a tree but couldn't get down. I said, 'Jump. I'll catch you.' 'What if you don't catch me?' she replied. 'I'll catch you. You must trust me.' Our eyes met and in a split second, both our different fears became one. 'Even I get scared at times,' I said. 'Scared of what?' 'Right now,' I said, 'I'm terrified that you won't trust me.' She smiled and, without any further hesitation, jumped, landing safely in my outstretched arms. She looked up at me and with unspoken words, we both said, 'We don't need to be afraid anymore. We trust each other.' It was a momentous moment in our lives.*

Real life stories are unbeatable. Chose the right story and the whole room will get goosebumps.

SAYING IT WITH HUMOUR

However, people can only take so much emotion. If they overdose, they will display the classic symptoms of sentiment fatigue: yawning, fidgeting, talking. The way to avoid this is to keep everyone happy by enlivening your sentimental reminiscences with little touches of humour.

Everyone loves a good gag. If you can find a *relevant* joke, you are onto a winner. It will relax the audience and you. Matching your choice of material to the nature of the guests is easy when the group all know each other. At wedding receptions this is often *not* the case, so you must choose your jokes with care.

Let's assume that only half the crowd know the best man, Dave, recently had a nasty bout of food poisoning while on his holidays. There is no need to bore the other half by bringing it up again in great detail. One simple gag will do the job:

> *It's fantastic to see Dave here today, fighting fit after his recent little problem. He went to Greece last month ... had the shish kebabs all week.*

Now *everyone* present should find that amusing – with the possible exception of Dave.

Choose your material with ingenuity and reconsider it with care. Does the humorous line arise naturally from the serious words that precede it? Does its punchline act as punctuation at the end of a paragraph so that you can embark smoothly on the next topic?

Look into the mirror
Any speaker who cannot laugh at himself leaves the job to others. Poke a little fun at yourself before you poke fun at anyone else.

> *What a panic yesterday evening. I heard (daughter) say to her mother, 'Mum, I've still got so much to do and I want everything to be perfect. I'm determined not to overlook even the most*

insignificant detail.' And her mother replied, 'Don't worry, love, I'll make sure your father is there.'

I remember the time I had a terrible throat. I couldn't eat, drink or even talk. When the doctor called, (daughter) said to him, 'Dad's got a drinking problem. What can you do to help him?'

Your daughter

Don't forget that it's her Big Day. And a few crass words can shatter it. Target any humour with extreme caution and care. Does she have a good sense of humour? If she's game for a laugh, then she's fair game.

(Daughter) had their joint credit card stolen last month. (Son-in-law) hasn't reported it as missing because the thief is taking less out each week than she was.'

(Daughter) is a wonderful daughter. For many years she has brightened up our lives ... usually by leaving all the lights on in the house when she goes out.

Your son-in-law

Once again, don't be too cruel and consider how he – and his family – is likely to react to a little gentle ribbing.

In many ways (son-in-law) has become like a son to me. He doesn't take any notice of what I say, he's always answering back and he is threatening to eat us out of house and home.

When (son-in-law) asked me for (daughter's) hand in marriage, I said, '(Son-in- law), do you think you're earning enough to support a family?' 'Yes,' he replied. 'Think carefully now,' I added, 'after all you know there are six of us.'

Your wife

Target a mild potshot in this direction only if you are sure it will be received by your good lady in the humorous spirit that you no doubt intended.

Being a romantic sort of girl, (wife) insisted on getting married in her grandmother's dress. She looked absolutely fabulous – but her poor old granny nearly froze to death.

As we entered this beautiful reception party, (wife) turned to me and said, 'You know, you don't seem quite as well dressed as when we got married 30 years ago.' I replied, 'Well I don't know why not, I'm wearing the same suit.'

Be positively insulting

Funnily enough, a teasing jibe and a sincere compliment often fit well together, each reinforcing the other in a kind of verbal synergy. The trick is to first set up a situation which you can exploit with a teasing remark, before turning this into a genuine compliment.

When she was 16, (daughter) joined the string section of the town orchestra. She practised at home day and night. For years she was always harping on about something or other (pause). Well, angels do, don't they?

So try to sugar your jokes with praise.

OFFERING SOME WORDS OF WISDOM

Rather than simply regurgitating the same old, clichéd pearl or trinket of wisdom that has been heard by a million other couples (and no doubt ignored by most of them), try to personalise any advice you may wish to proffer. Give the bride and groom (and everyone else in the room) the benefit of any relevant life lessons you have learned through success or failure. How can they apply this to *their* lives?

> *Last year, for our Pearl Anniversary, some old friends gave us a DVD copy of the original cine recording of our wedding. We were thrilled. They told us we'd have to be able to lip read to know what was going on because there was no sound. But that didn't matter at all because we remember the day like it was yesterday. My father-in-law, the late (his name), a true Yorkshireman, made a lovely speech and told us to always remember that money comes first and last. You've got to make it first, and then make it last. That advice has served us well for over thirty years and I now pass on his wise words, with immense thanks, to the next generation.*

ADDING A SPARKLE TO YOUR SPEECH

There are a number of ways you can make your speech special and spellbinding. No-one is expecting you to be a great raconteur. However, there are a few tricks of the trade that can help give any speech a lyrical, almost magical quality.

Using words to be said, not read

Most people know how to write something intended to be *read*, far fewer know how to write something intended to be *said*. Indeed, many are unaware there is even a difference. We are used to writing things to be read. Such everyday written communication is known as *text*. What we are not so used to doing is speaking our written words out loud. Writing intended to be spoken and heard is known as *script*.

Every effective speaker must recognise that there are very important differences between text and script, namely:

Text	Script
is a journey at the reader's pace	is a journey at the speaker's pace
can be re-read, if necessary	is heard once, and only once
can be read in any order	is heard in the order it is spoken.

Therefore, you must prepare and present a speech for an audience who *cannot* listen at their own pace; who *cannot* ask you to repeat parts they did not hear or understand; and who *cannot* choose the order in which to consider your words.

We seem subconsciously to understand the best words and phrases when we *speak*, but we seem to loose the knack when we *write* a script. Consider how the same sentiment might be conveyed by a writer, first using text and then script:

Text

The meaning of marriage is not to be found in church services or in romantic novels or films. We have no right to expect a happy ending. The meaning of marriage is to be found in all the effort that is required to make a marriage succeed. You need to get to know your partner and thereby get to know yourself.

Script

The meaning of marriage isn't to be found in wedding bells...it isn't the stuff of Mills and Boon romances...there is no happy ever after, No, the meaning of marriage is in the trying and it's about learning about someone else...and through that learning about yourself.

The lesson is clear – speak your words out loud before you commit them to paper. You will find that each element, each phrase, each sentence will build from what has gone before. Instinctively, you will take your listeners from the *known* to the *unknown*; from the *general* to the *specific*; from the *present* to the *future*.

As a speechmaker, you must:

▶ think like a listener, and
▶ write like a talker.

Using warm words

Words are powerful. They conjure images, evoke emotions and trigger responses deep within us so we react, often without knowing why. So-called *warm* words make us feel secure and comfortable, while *cold* words leave us uneasy and unsure. Writer Henry James said the two most beautiful words in the English language are *summer afternoon*, because they evoke just the right emotions.

***Love** fills your life with **happiness**, gives you **strength** and **grows** beyond you. You feel **warmed** by their presence even if they're away. Distance cannot separate you. Near or far, you **know** they are **yours** and you can wait for them. A **successful** relationship*

grows *between two people who really **like** as well as **love** each other.*

Painting word pictures

Today people spend more time *watching* TV or films than *listening* to the radio. They are used to visual images so you must give your speech a graphic quality by not telling the story, but by painting word pictures that allow your audience's imagination to take over.

> *(Daughter) and I loved going to gran's on a Saturday. Tea was lovely, fish and chips that gran didn't fetch from the shop but cooked herself, cream meringues and chocolate éclairs, tinned peaches with evaporated milk, the whole lot washed down with fizzy lemonade.*

Can't you just feel that gassy pop getting up your nose?

Using figurative language

Try to make your speech colourful and original. Similes and metaphors are particularly useful devices. A **simile** is a figure of speech, usually introduced by *like* or *as*, that **compares** one thing to another.

> *She was simmering like a corked volcano.*

A **metaphor** does not so much compare as **transform** one thing to another.

> *Marriage. Ever since humans gathered together in caves, they – we – have displayed a basic instinct for becoming couples. Your man and your woman. Your Romeo and your Juliet. Your yin and your yang. It's as natural as his and hers bath towels. If the life of*

humankind were music, they would all be duets. It's been a bit of a musical day one way and another. Violins in harmony with cellos. (Daughter) in harmony with (son-in-law). The past in harmony with the future. And, as the Bard of Avon put it: 'If music be the food of love, play on'.

Remembering rhythm

A good speech should attract and hold listeners as a magnet attracts and holds iron filings. Here are three simple techniques that can turn your words into music in an audience's ear.

The rule of three

Three is a magic number. People love to hear speakers talk to the beat of three. The effect of three words, three phrases or three sentences is powerful and memorable.

> *We wish you fun and excitement for today . . . hopes and dreams for tomorrow . . . and love and happiness forever.*

Parallel sentences

This takes the rule of three one stage further by beginning each sentence with the identical words. Sentences that are parallel add a rhythmic beauty and help an audience anticipate and follow your thoughts.

> *Marriage is a celebration of love. Marriage is a celebration of life. Marriage is a celebration of joy.*

Alliteration

The recurrence of sounds and syllables, usually at the beginning of words, can help create just the right mood.

*Water your garden with **friendship**, **faith** and **favour**. And then watch it grow. You deserve a garden of love.*

Weaving in a couple of quotations

Everyone enjoys hearing a particularly witty or wise turn of phrase or apt quotation. However, very few quotes will be received with knee-slapping belly laughter or will cause a lump in the throat. Their merit usually lies in their encapsulation of a truth, a smart observation or a humorous example. Use them in moderation and keep them relevant to the personal circumstances and background of the couple.

I am reminded of a verse from HMS Pinafore: *'When he was a lad he served his term. As an office boy to an Attorney's firm. He cleaned the windows and he swept the floor. And he polished the handle of the big front door. He polished up that handle so carefullee. That now he's the Ruler of the Queen's Navee'* – *well, almost, anyway.*

BEGINNING AND ENDING IN STYLE

People remember best what they hear first and what they hear last. Think of your opening and closing words as the verbal bookends of your speech. They must be strong enough to hold and support everything that comes between them.

Hooking the audience

Successful speechmakers often ponder, consciously and unconsciously, for days over their opening words. They know that the first few sentences of their speech set the course for success or failure: a good start sets you plain sailing, a poor one makes you sail against the wind.

Ladies and Gentlemen, 'We cannot fully enjoy life until someone we love enjoys it with us.' Not my words, I'm afraid, but how I agree with them . . .

Adding a topical reference

In the early part of your speech, it's a good idea to throw in a line or two about something funny, amusing or poignant that has happened earlier in the day. Your guests will know this reference could not have been planned and this ploy will help give the whole speech a feeling of spontaneity.

And what about that magnificent young cellist? She has attracted so much favourable comment that I simply have to give her a special mention.

Ending on a high

Try to end with a flourish. Your concluding remark should be what the high note is to an aria: the incandescence that triggers applause. If you can wrap up your speech perfectly, you will inject that ultimate bit of magic.

Marriage is a constant journey of understanding, fun, sorrow, forgiveness, laughter, sharing. In short, it is a journey of life, a journey of love. May your journey be a long one, filled with joy.

Making that toast

All you need to do now is add a few words after your big finish.

Ladies and Gentlemen, please stand, raise your glasses and drink a toast with me to the health and happiness of (son-in-law and daughter).

To (son-in-law and daughter)!

If you have two children, be careful not to marry the wrong one off, or marry them to one another. Let's say your children are Jane and Barbara and Barbara is getting married. You'll be used to putting their names together and it would be all too easy to fall into the trap of saying, 'Please raise your glasses to Jane and Barbara!' rather than, '...to Steve and Barbara!' Your family may think this is quite a laugh, but Steve's may not be quite so accommodating.

Bracketing your speech

This is a device usually associated with seasoned pros. It is designed not only to grab an audience's attention at the *start* of a speech, but also – and at the same time – set-up a situation that can be exploited at the *end*.

The idea of bracketing is to present your speech as a satisfying whole, not merely a series of thoughts. reminiscences and humorous asides. Here is an example of a possible pair of brackets. The words used at the end will include some which were planted clearly at the start.

Set-up

On such a day as this I hope I can be forgiven for indulging in a little daydreaming – both reminiscing about the past and predicting the future. Today we celebrate a marriage, the union of my daughter (daughter) and her new husband (son-in-law)...

Pay off

Now all this daydreaming must stop. It is time to move on. At the end of all my reminiscing, I've come to these inescapable conclusions: (wife) and I did a lot for (daughter)...but she did even more for us. Of course, she will always be our dear daughter, but there is no doubt in our minds that the time is now right to entrust her to (son-in-law's) loving care. And knowing (son-in-law) as we do, we are certain it will be very, very good care...(followed by the toast).

Notice how the repetition of the words *daydreaming* and *reminiscing*, together with the repetition of your daughter's and son-in-law's names, helps the open-and-closed nature of the brackets and provides a pleasing and memorable symmetry.

KEEPING IT FLOWING

Have you noticed how entertainers, politicians and news readers move easily and unobtrusively from one topic to another? Like them, you can keep your speech flowing naturally by making use of a few of these simple devices.

Bridges

A bridge is word that alerts the audience that you are changing direction or moving to a new thought.

And she took the job in London. **Meanwhile** *other developments were taking place...*

Triggers

A trigger is a repetition of the same word or phrase to link one topic with another.

That's what (daughter) **was like** *at school. Now I'll tell you what she* **was like** *at college...*

Rhetorical questions

These are questions which do not require an answer. As well as serving as a way of keeping things flowing, they also allow you to pass on information to people without insulting the intelligence of those already in the know.

> *What can I tell you about a girl who won the school prize for chemistry, represented the county at netball and passed her driving test – at the sixth attempt?*

Flashbacks

A sudden shift to the past is a far more interesting way of linking topics than simply listing events chronologically.

> *Today she is the confident woman-about-town you see before you.* ***But five years ago*** *she wasn't like that...*

Identifiers

An identifier is a word or phrase that keeps cropping up throughout a speech to help create the impression of a coherent whole, not merely a series of thoughts, observations and reminiscences. It also reinforces the audience's group identity.

> *Look at* ***our*** *(not* ***the****) beautiful bride...*

> ***We*** *(not* ***I****) wish them well...*

Pauses

This is a non-verbal way of showing your audience that you have finished one section of your speech and are about to move on to another.

Physical movements

If you turn to your daughter, the guests will know you are going to talk to her, or about her.

Quotations, jokes or stories

Any of these can also serve as an excellent link. Here a man-on-the-bus gag links a personal compliment about your daughter's good manners with a more general observation that everyone has played their part in making this a day to remember.

> *(Daughter) always shows good old-fashioned courtesy to her fellow human beings. A rare attribute today, I'm sure you'll agree. When she was on the bus last week she stood up to give an elderly gentleman her seat. He was so surprised, he fainted. When he came to he said, 'Thank you,' and (daughter) fainted. Well I'm delighted to say there has been absolutely no shortage of courtesy here today. You've all been great. Things could not have gone better...*

PREPARING YOUR SCRIPT

The best talkers are those who are the most natural. They are easy, fluent, friendly and amusing. No script for them. How could there be? They are talking only to us and basing what they say on our reactions as they go along. For most of us, however, this sort of performance is an aspiration rather than a description. Our tongues are not so honeyed and our words are less than winged. We need a script.

But what sort of script? Cards? Notes? A speech written out in full? There is no right way of doing it. Here is a simple method favoured by many speakers:

▶ Write the speech out **in full**.

▶ **Memorise** the opening and closing lines and **familiarise** yourself with the rest of the speech.

▶ **Summarise** the speech on one card, or one sheet of paper using **key words** to remind you of your sequence of stories, reminiscences and so forth.

The great advantage of this technique is that you won't forget huge chunks of your speech and you will come across as a natural and spontaneous speaker because you will be using your own words and phrases, not simply reciting a prepared speech.

The ideal approach, then, is to appear extemporaneous, to present a speech that is a happy compromise between one that is read word for word or learnt by heart and one that is completely impromptu and unprepared. The key is to prepare the substance of what you will say, but not the precise words you will use to convey it. As actors are taught: 'Dig deep to fly high and then throw it all away.'

PUTTING IT ALL TOGETHER

Traditionally, the father of the bride's speech is the first address, followed by the groom, best man and, increasingly, the bride. Nowadays there may well be some variations. For example, the father may make a joint speech with his wife, he may share the stage with a stepdad, he may simply thank people for coming and then offer a toast, or he may show a short film or some photographs of his daughter as a child.

To meet people's expectations, your address should contain the following broad sections and messages.

- ▶ Hook and officially welcome guests on behalf of your family.
- ▶ Give a special mention to any close friends or family who were unable to attend.
- ▶ Thank everyone involved in the organisation (and funding).
- ▶ Express your pride in your daughter.
- ▶ Welcome your son-in-law into the family.
- ▶ Welcome his family.
- ▶ Reminisce about your daughter's pre-wedding years.
- ▶ Pay a tribute to your wife.
- ▶ Proffer some personalised advice to the couple.
- ▶ Wish them success and happiness for the future.
- ▶ Propose a toast to the bride and groom.

When planning your speech, the best advice is to start early. Your most original and useful ideas will tend to occur at the oddest of times, so always keep a notebook handy. Try to create an interior 'film' in the listeners' head through the words you speak and the mental images you create. Then forget about your speech for a couple of days. Allow it to simmer so you can return to it with a fresh perspective

When you re-visit it, read it out loud. Right away you will be aware of the parts that are spot on, the parts that need a little tweaking, and the parts that are simply not worth including. Once you're happy with each of the various sections of your speech, try to link them together naturally so the whole thing flows gracefully from beginning to end.

Let's now prepare a first draft of a father of the bride's speech, following the traditional structure. Of course, you may decide to change the order a little, or combine one or more sections, or perhaps even add something entirely new. The important thing is to make your speech unique, personal and relevant. In the same way as no woman wants to go to a wedding with the same dress as anyone else, a father of the bride should pride himself by not going to a wedding with the same speech as anyone else.

Hook and officially welcome guests on behalf of your family

'Love is a great force in life, it is indeed the greatest of all things.' So said E.M. Forster, and E.M. knew what he was talking about.

Ladies and Gentlemen, this is a truly historic day! This day, the 28th of June, will always be remembered for three world famous events. Henry VIII was born back in 1491, the British Lions roared to an amazing series win against South Africa in 1997, and on this day in 200X, (son-in-law) married (daughter)!

I'd like to start by welcoming, on behalf of (wife, daughter and son-in-law), the guests from both our families. It's wonderful to be surrounded by so many friends and family who have been so important to us during our lives. By your presence here today, you show friendship and love, and bring even greater joy to us all. Happiness and joy ring in the air.

A special word of welcome must go to Hans and Gretel, our dear friends who have flown in all the way from Holland to be with us today. It's amazing what some people will do for a free meal. Hans, I've got a couple of bottles of schnapps in. Thank you both so much for coming – dank U wel.

Well I don't know what the weather is like back in old Amsterdam, but it can't be any nicer than this. We have been so lucky that the sun has shone down upon us throughout this very special day. It's been an incredibly bright start for what is sure to be an incredibly bright future for you both, as man and wife.

Give a special mention to any close friends or family who were unable to attend

Unfortunately, Ian and Mary couldn't be with us today because Ian is unwell. I'm sure we all wish him a speedy and full recovery. I spoke to him yesterday and he told me to pass on their very best wishes and to say they would be raising a glass or two to you both this evening.

Sadly, as many of you will know, Uncle Robert passed away earlier this year. Although we all miss Bob terribly, we can all rejoice in the fact that he would have been absolutely delighted that (son-in-law) and (daughter) have now tied the knot. In a sense I feel he is celebrating here with us today because, like me, Bob knew you two were made for each other.

Thank everyone involved in the organisation (and funding)

Now weddings don't just happen. They take a fantastic amount of work and organisation. As most of you will already be aware, today's events were planned and co-ordinated with panache and precision by (daughter). Without her things would not have run so smoothly or have been so fantastic and memorable. Over the last year she has displayed the patience of Job, the wisdom of Solomon and the organisational skills of, well (daughter). I know I'm speaking on behalf of you all when I say thank you so very, very much. You couldn't have made a better job of it.

Express your pride in your daughter

You know, today really belongs to her – and, of course, to her co-star (son-in- law). We are both so proud of (daughter). She has the gift of finding joy everywhere and of leaving it behind when she goes. If she had a pound for every smile she's put on a face, she'd be a millionaire. And talk about being sensitive and caring. Last week she had to tell her class who'd been chosen for the school play – and who hadn't been. Those who hadn't been given a part were told they'd been given the vital job of sitting in the audience and clapping and cheering. Everyone was over the moon. That's what I call being diplomatic. Some of our politicians could learn a lesson or two from you. I'm so proud of you and I want the world to know it. You deserve such a perfect day as this.

Welcome your son-in-law into the family

And what about this debonair young man at her side? Well, quite simply, over the last few months we've come to the inescapable conclusion that he's exactly the type of person we'd always hoped (daughter) would marry: a man who knows where he's going in life and how he's going to get there. We're so impressed that he's such a hard-working, dependable and trustworthy man with absolutely immaculate tastes. After all, he supports United and he chose (daughter), didn't he? From the very first moment we saw them together, we knew they were the perfect match. Their devotion was obvious. Their affection radiant. Their love exploded like fireworks. (Son-in-law), we're so pleased to formally welcome you into the (your surname) clan.

Welcome his family

And an equally warm welcome goes to (son-in-law's) parents, (their first names). We've all got to know each other really well over the last few months and I like to think we've grown into good friends. Of course, marriage is not only about finding the right person, it is about being the right person. What doubles our joy is the fact that, like us, you are certain that your son has found his perfect partner in life.

Reminisce about your daughter's pre-wedding years

Where were you on 28th June, 1983? In my case, I was at Anytown Hospital maternity ward. And, not surprisingly, so was (wife). When a first child is born there are really three births – the birth of the child, the birth of the mother and the birth of the father. The entire world looked different to me from the moment she was born.

(Daughter) was always a very special daughter – kind, considerate, loving – and a source of great pride and joy as we watched her grow. We shared her birth cries and smiled through her first steps, her first words, her first giggles. We beamed through school concerts, sports' days and birthdays. We shared laughter and tears. Every passing year gave us events to remember and memories to cherish. As she grew, I recorded every special memory in my heart.

I remember one warm, quiet, sunny afternoon when we were sitting hand in hand in the park. Not talking. Not doing anything really. A neighbour strolled by and said, 'So you're not busy today, (your name).' I smiled back politely, thinking to myself: I'm extremely busy, busy making memories.

When she was about ten she made her first little cake. It was a brilliant first effort. A few days later she made four individual cakes for the family only to find there were five of us home for tea that day. Immediately she announced that she never really cared for cakes herself. That's the kind of person she is. (Daughter) not only makes the best cakes, she makes the best memories too.

During her early teenage years, we had an old biscuit tin in which we used to exchange letters and notes. 'Dad, I'm in the school play'; 'Dad, I got an A in Maths'; 'Dad, I love you.' It was wonderful. But imagine my horror the day I read that I was going to be a grandfather. What should I do? What should I say? That evening my unremitting panic turned to unmitigated relief when (daughter) told me her dog Suzy was going to have puppies.

When she went off to Uni, the tin got put away. Then, about a year ago, it mysteriously re-appeared. This time my message read: 'Dad, I'm getting married.' It was fantastic news. I wanted to shout for joy. In fact I did. I just hope it won't be too long before I get another little note saying I really am going to be a granddad.

Pay a tribute to your wife

The only trouble about being a grandfather, of course, is that you have to be married to a grandmother. Only joking, (wife). But I really would like to take this opportunity to say I am the luckiest man in the world, not only to be blessed with such a wonderful daughter, but also to be married to the best wife and best mother in the world. It's not that she does any one thing that makes her the best wife in the world, it's all the little things she does for us. It's the understanding and the acceptance and the way she takes care of everything. It's the way she treats me, forgives me, puts up with me – and loves me. (Son-in-law), they say as a daughter gets older, she turns out to be more and more like her mother. If this happens to (daughter), you can ask for no more in life.

Proffer some personalised advice to the couple

Now it is customary on an occasion such as this for the father of the bride to pass on some words of wisdom about love and marriage. Well just before I got married back in 1980, my father gave us some invaluable advice which I now pass on to you two today. Dad produced a large sheet of white paper just like this one (hold up a sheet of paper) and drew a tiny black dot in the centre (do the same). 'What do you see?' he asked. 'A little spot,' we replied. 'Anything else?' We looked hard at the paper and then at each other with blank expressions. 'You see a little black dot which represents the problems that you may face in the future. What you have both missed is all the white space that makes up the rest of the page. Good things can easily be ignored and taken for granted simply because they are so obvious. Always look beyond any tiny black spots and appreciate that huge white space.'

Wish them success and happiness for the future

You are lucky people. Lucky to have found your best friend; lucky to be in love; lucky to know deep in your hearts that you're ready to share your lives together. A successful marriage involves falling in love many, many times – but each time with the same person. I am confident that you both have all the qualities needed to achieve this. Not only that, you both have the sense of humour, love and support for one another necessary to help you through any tiny black spots you may encounter – and the courage and determination to make sure white space is soon restored.

Propose a toast to the bride and groom

Ladies and Gentlemen, today has been blessed with spontaneity, the laughter of family and friends and – most importantly – the deep love between man and wife. Oh yes, and the excitement and joy of a very happy, very proud father.

There are only two lasting bequests parents can hope to give their children – one of these is roots and the other is wings. (Daughter), I believe over the years we have given you strong roots. Today, (wife) and I know the time is right for you to fly away from the nest with (son-in-law).

Ladies and Gentlemen – Friends, it is my pleasant and proud duty to propose a toast to the happy couple ... to the love birds ... to (son-in-law and daughter).

To (son-in-law and daughter)!

REHEARSING YOUR SPEECH

Why do some actors freeze or fumble on the opening night and then pick up a Lawrence Olivier award six months later? It is the fear of unfamiliarity. As the days, weeks and months go by, the fear abates and the quality of performance improves.

Words become more familiar. Awkward juxtapositions are smoothed out. You suddenly think of a way of saying a stuffy sentence in a more straightforward and colloquial style. Some speakers like to rehearse, isolated and unheard, in a distant room, with or without a mirror. Others perform their speeches again and again to a sympathetic spouse or friend, either encouraging suggestions from them or requiring nothing more than a repeated hearing to ease away their inhibitions.

Developing your comfort zone

Rehearse the beginning and ending of your speech to be spot on – and make sure you get the groom's name right. Rehearse the body of your speech not to be perfect, but to be *comfortable*. Audiences don't expect you to be perfect, but they *need* you to be comfortable. If you're not comfortable, they *cannot* be comfortable either. And if they are not comfortable, they *cannot* be fully receptive to your words of wit and wisdom, however hard they may try.

PART 3

FOUR PARTIES
AND A WEDDING

Pre-wedding Celebrations

'I am thankful for the mess to clean after a party because it means I have been surrounded by friends.' (Nancie J. Carmody)

Any excuse for a party? The announcement of a wedding gives party animals the ideal opportunity to let their hair down. It also gives people from both families a great chance to get to know each other. While there is really no limit to the number of events that can be organised before a wedding (the 'big one', of course, coming *after* the ceremony), there are usually three pre-wedding get-togethers which you *may* be involved in. They are:

► the engagement party
► the stag do
► the rehearsal dinner.

As with most wedding-related etiquette, over recent years traditional hosting roles and responsibilities have become blurred. Nowadays, a party may be hosted by your family, by the groom's family, by both families jointly, or perhaps by the happy couple themselves. As you are unlikely to be involved in arranging the stag do, and because the rehearsal dinner should be a fairly straightforward affair, this chapter will concentrate largely, though not exclusively, on the engagement party.

ARRANGING THE ENGAGEMENT PARTY

An engagement party can serve a number of useful purposes. It can be a great way of introducing both sets of parents to each other over an informal meal. It can also be an opportunity to bring family, friends and colleagues together under the same roof. And if your family is well known for hosting parties, it can be a memorable way of announcing the engagement to an unsuspecting world.

Planning the party

Try not to go over the top with the engagement party; you want to ensure that the wedding day does not pale or fall flat in comparison to the party. Venue, food and entertainment should be tailored to your guests and their preferences. Caterers and organised entertainment will bump up the cost, but leave you with a lot less to do. Cost out the various options and choose the best solution that is within your budget and appropriate for the occasion. Initially you will need to ask yourself three key questions, namely: *When?*, *Where?* and *How many?*

➤ **When?**

Unless children are to be included, most people would agree that an evening party is the best option. Try to arrange it to be held within a month or two of you hearing the happy news, especially if it is to be a short engagement. You do not want it to take place too close to the hen and stag dos, or to the main reception. Before you finalise the date, confirm that you and your wife, your daughter and her fiancé, and his parents have no prior engagements on that day. Make sure your guests know about it well in advance, so they can keep it free.

▶ **Where?**

An engagement party can simply be a get-together in a family home, in which case it may well be held at your house. Alternatively, it can be a more formal affair in a hall with caterers or a private function room in a hotel, restaurant or pub. What would make the occasion special for your daughter and her fiancé? Would they prefer a formal sit-down meal or an informal do?

▶ **How many?**

Will it be a small and intimate family gathering or perhaps a big party for all their friends? Remember that an engagement party is *not* a dress rehearsal for the big day. As the name suggests, it's a party. So don't feel that you have to invite everyone who will be invited to the wedding. However, anyone that you do ask should also be asked to the wedding. They would feel extremely insulted to have been invited to the engagement party and then to be missed off the wedding guest list.

Sending out the invitations

If you are hosting the party, then the invitations should come from you. Send them out one to two months in advance. Do you issue formal invitations or just call up friends and invite them? This is up to you and the sort of party you are having. If it's to be a dinner at a hotel or private house, a printed invitation with an RSVP would be appropriate. If you are meeting at a bar or restaurant or having an informal gathering at your home, a phone call or quick email would be fine.

I have a theme

Some couples like to give the party a theme: Gangsters and Molls,

Fabulous Fifties Rock & Roll, Superheroes – anything they like really. Having a theme party helps break the ice and generally adds an element of frivolity to the occasion.

A themed engagement party is no more difficult to co-ordinate than a traditional event, depending on the desired level of detail. The key is for each of the engagement party ideas to be *integrated*: invitations, food, music, decorations and activities.

Keeping everyone happy

Engagement parties invariably involve guests of different ages and varying backgrounds. Regardless of the degree of formality, it is important to keep everyone involved and entertained throughout the proceedings. The more informal the do, the more activities – fun games, quizzes, re-enactment of the proposal – you may wish to include. As you plan the event, try to imagine what different guests would appreciate having laid on.

Making the announcement

If you can contain your excitement long enough to break the happy news at the party, then make that announcement the focal point of the evening. Choose a time when most of your guests have arrived, but before anyone has had the opportunity to drink a little too much. Get something musical to herald the big moment. If there is a band, a roll on the drums would be perfect. Otherwise, a loud blast of something fitting on the CD should get people's attention.

If the guests are already aware of the engagement, be prepared to say a few congratulatory, upbeat, optimistic words instead. You don't need to say very much; keep your powder dry for the reception.

Doing your own thing

You may decide to hold the party at home. That's fine so long as you appreciate what you are taking on. Even if you go down this route, you may still consider it is worth including one or two professional add-ons, such as catering or crockery hire. As with most things in life, it's important to plan these things well in advance.

Make a list of lists

Write a list of every party job you can think of. Get as much done as you can before the event: clean out the fridge to give you more space for party food and drinks, think about what can be prepared and frozen in advance. Consider anything and everything that doesn't need to be done on the day itself. Try to arrange as much help at the party as you can. You'll be inviting people to spend their valuable time with you; you owe it to them to have plenty of time to talk to them.

Food for thought

Even though the party will be at a private family home, it's well worth considering bringing in outside catering, especially if a lot of people will be attending. Catering for a large group of people is very different from catering for your immediate family. This will also leave you and your family free to enjoy yourselves.

Arrange a meeting to talk to your caterers, so you can explain exactly what you want and avoid disappointment on the day. Food is a matter of personal taste and your guests won't necessarily like what you like, so choose your menu with care. Remember to always include vegetarian alternatives.

A little libation

Get some bottles in when they are on special offer. Remember to include some champers or cava to open when the announcement is made. And don't forget that you'll also need to provide a selection of non-alcoholic drinks. Put plenty of bin liners around the house so people will have somewhere to dispose of their empties. Clear away any valuables which might get damaged.

Entertainment

Do you want organised entertainment, or simply to create an opportunity for people to meet and socialise? At an informal party, you'll probably get away with a CD player. When it comes to the choice of music, remember to include something for everyone.

Their presence or their presents?

At an informal occasion, it is unlikely guests will bring gifts other then a bottle of wine, some chocolates or perhaps a DVD. Remind your daughter not to open any presents at the do as this may embarrass people who have not brought anything for them. Your daughter may prefer to ask the guests not to bring anything other than themselves. Nonetheless, *you* may decide to get them a surprise gift to mark the occasion.

If you are hosting a more formal event, your guests will probably bring something more substantial, unless they are specifically requested not to. Engagement parties can result in a lot of unwanted presents that sometimes may not be returnable to shops. For this reason, your daughter may wish to produce a modest list for her favourite shop, or perhaps could ask for vouchers. Guests often assume they have to call the bride's mother for information about this, so it would be useful for your wife to have a copy of this list.

Lights, camera, action
Many people are likely to bring cameras with them. You might decide to provide them with some disposable ones too. Collectively they can provide your daughter with a unique record of the event, both posed and unposed, in a mix of colour and black and white. And if you have a camcorder, or access to one, why not use it?

Hiring party staff

Whether or not you have employed the services of a wedding co-ordinator, engaging the right professionals can really take the stress out of things and help ensure things run, well, professionally.

Setting your budget
Some people first decide how much they *want* to spend per head and then calculate their overall budget; others begin with an overall budget and then work out how much they can *afford* to spend per head. Clearly, the second method keeps a far tighter control over your cash.

Put your management accountant's hat on and think about both your *fixed* costs (such as the hire of the room) and your *variable* costs (such as the number of guests). Include everything and then break it down into parts: food, drink, music, decorations. As we saw in Chapter 5, there are many ways of cost-cutting. Talk everything through in detail with your various suppliers.

Finding the right people
Word of mouth remains the best way to choose the best professionals. Talk to your friends. Have they been to a party that had superb staff, catering, music, decorations? If so, ring the host and get their numbers.

Then check out www.reviewcentre.com for reviews of the suppliers of many wedding-related services, such as caterers, entertainers and party decorators.

Caterers

You're looking for someone who can produce quality in quantity. If you're going to be serving up food to people, it's important to find out what it tastes like first. Ask your prospective caterer to make up a selection of food so you can decide whether it's good value for money or not.

Entertainers

For a big event, it's worth hiring a professional DJ, or perhaps a singer or band. Ask for a list of songs from their repertoire and make sure you listen to them before you book them. Choose entertainers who will suit the tastes of all your guests; a band capable of playing background music and an all-out party set, guaranteed to get everyone up and dancing.

Whoever you choose, don't pay fully in advance, or they may not even turn up. Ask them to arrive a little earlier than you need them, just to be on the safe side. And then keep them happy; you might be asking them to play an encore at the end of the night. That means giving them a *few* drinks and *lots* of food and loud applause.

Party decorators

There are brilliant party decorators and florists out there. Just make sure you don't get carried away or go over the top. Choose seasonal flowers and be aware that your decorations will probably have been pulled down by the end of the evening anyway.

Making those bookings

Don't be frightened to tell people when you have been given lower quotes elsewhere; they may be willing to match or even undercut them. Then book up your caterers, musicians and party decorators – and hire any necessary tableware, cutlery, furniture, linen, glassware, cake stands, buffet tables, kitchen equipment, patio and garden furniture as early as possible. The bigger the do, the longer the notice they will need.

Listen to the experts

Always listen to the staff you've employed. They've probably had loads of experience in the party game and will know what works and what doesn't. If you're willing to take a reasonably flexible, 'ad hoc' approach, they can come up with some exciting ideas which you may never even have contemplated.

Throwing a surprise party

If nothing has yet been organised, or perhaps even discussed, you could take the bull by the horns and arrange a surprise do. For this to work, you will need a confederate, someone in on your cunning plan. One of you needs to get the happy couple to the party, while the other keeps the guests in order until they arrive. You will also need to ensure absolute secrecy. Visit your chosen venue and explain to them the nature of the party. If possible, book a private room where the guests can gather. Let the establishment know that you and the guests of honour will be arriving a little later than the main party.

When you send out invitations or email their friends and relatives, make it absolutely clear that your daughter will not be expecting them to be there. Implore them to keep this to themselves, whether or not they intend to come.

Tell your daughter that, as an engagement gift, you have booked them a romantic table for two and that you will be pleased to act as chauffeur for the evening. When the three of you arrive, escort them into the hired room where they will be greeted by a chorus of 'Surprise! Surprise!', a shower of confetti and party noisemakers.

Hosting the perfect engagement party
When it comes to hosting the perfect party, there are some rules that will ensure everything runs smoothly throughout.

- ▶ Welcome everyone as they arrive.
- ▶ Offer them drinks.
- ▶ Overestimate the food and drink required.
- ▶ Arrange for the food to be served soon after all the guests have arrived.
- ▶ Provide a variety of food, music and entertainment.
- ▶ Mingle.
- ▶ Encourage people to talk to one another.
- ▶ Keep everyone occupied.
- ▶ Create as much space as possible.
- ▶ Provide comfortable seating for disabled and elderly guests.
- ▶ Be a great host.

If you stick to these simple guidelines, it is sure to be a party to remember – and for the right reasons.

ATTENDING THE STAG DO
You may well not be invited to this pre-wedding bash. After all it is an important rite of passage that the groom is supposed to share with peers, not parents. However, if you are asked think very carefully before you accept. How would you be likely to react to

certain revelations and disclosures of a personal nature brought on by your future son-in-law's copious consumption of cognac? If you could handle that – and if you are a middle-youthed Ozzy Osbourne hellraiser who still likes to let his hair down, even though he hasn't got any – you would probably have a great time with the lads. But if that's not really you, it's probably better to start thinking up a prior engagement.

REMEMBERING THE REHEARSAL DINNER

It is becoming common practice for the main players to attend a rehearsal dinner after their final run through at the wedding site. This meal is usually booked in advance by the happy couple. The atmosphere should be very informal. So just relax and enjoy yourself. However, once again, do prepare a few choice words in advance just in case you are called upon to make a short speech or propose a toast.

And finally ...
Some couples budget for a pre-wedding get-together of guests immediately after the rehearsal dinner, especially if their engagement party was a small, intimate, family affair. Typically this would take place at some local nightspot. By this means, people from both families get to know each other before the reception. Instant recognition on the day avoids awkward and icy introductions and facilitates an easy transition from ceremony to revelry.

Ceremonial Duties

'Life isn't a matter of milestone, but of moments.' (Rose Kennedy)

On the wedding day there are a number of traditional duties which you may be expected to fulfil. Be aware that there may be some variations to these according to the structure of your family and the wishes of your daughter. Maybe she wants both her father and stepfather to walk her down the aisle, or perhaps she wants her mother to do it. Whatever her choices, unless you feel so uncomfortable that you feel compelled to speak out, try to understand her reasoning and motives – and respect and accept her decisions.

Your responsibilities on the day may also be affected, to some degree at least, by the religious or secular nature of the ceremony. Civil ceremonies in stately homes, other prestigious buildings, and hotels and restaurants can often be more flexible than religious ones. This gives your daughter some scope to make a few variations to the service. However, they will still have certain rules and regulations which must be followed.

YOUR TASKS THROUGHOUT THE DAY

Early on in the morning of the Big Day, all the mundane, everyday activities of normal life will cease and everything will be geared to the time of the ceremony. The bride, her mother and her bridesmaids will probably be virtually unapproachable and all the ordinary things that need to be done – phone calls to be made, dog to be walked – fall to you either to do yourself or to make sure someone else does them. In short, you become a sort of project manager but without the authority to change anything you feel isn't right.

Once the hairdressers, beauticians, dressmakers and other advisers have come and gone, the bride will stand ready to dazzle all around her. While you may have some traditional duties to perform before the ceremony, your main focus at this stage should be to help her approach her wedding with joy rather than stress. You also need to recognise and respond to the emotional turmoil your wife will be experiencing. But before you can do these things, you first need to understand what *you* are feeling – and why you are feeling it.

Acknowledging how you feel

Men are generally not brought up or encouraged to express their feelings – even to themselves. While it is not a good idea to lie on the proverbial psychiatrist's couch and express every innermost doubt and fear, it is still important to recognise how you are feeling and why you are feeling it. It is perfectly natural to be (a little) sad. Don't bottle things up. Acknowledge that this is a momentous day in your life too. You won't be able to support your daughter effectively until you have got to grips with your own emotions.

Supporting your daughter

This is probably the most important day in your daughter's life, so far. Is it really surprising that she's a little nervous? Some last minute concerns will be logistical: 'What if there is a problem with the food?' Others will be psychological. The same girl who was so laid back over the last few months may suddenly no longer want to be the centre of all this attention. Yet the nervousness experienced by most brides-to-be usually stems from the realisation that life can never be quite the same again.

You should be able to reassure her that everything has been thoroughly planned and you have contingency plans in place should anything go awry. Remind her that it is perfectly natural to feel this way. She needs to recognise that nerves are simply the body's way of preparing for something special.

This is a time to be upbeat and positive. It is her Big Day. Everyone is on her side. She is about to begin an exciting new chapter of her life alongside the man she loves. Tell her she's not losing a father, she's gaining a husband.

She's got pre-match nerves

It is not unusual for a bride-to-be to have some last minute jitters. Suddenly the realisation that this is an enormous step dawns upon her. Marriage is a commitment, a binding promise to spend the rest of her life with this one man. If she has never had *any* doubts about this, she has either been extremely lucky or she has not thought about the implications seriously enough.

So how should you react when she comes crying on your shoulder, possibly on the Big Day itself? Well firstly, never lie or say things just because you think she wants to hear them. If she does marry and it all goes wrong, who do you think will get the blame? The important thing is to establish what the fundamental problem is. If it's about something trivial, it will probably soon blow over. If it's about a more basic conflict, either inside her head or with her fiancé, for the marriage to succeed that conflict must be resolved either by a mutually agreeable compromise or by a change in attitude or behaviour.

Encourage your daughter to talk to you – and, more importantly, to talk to her fiancé, even at this late stage. If he really loves her, he will try to understand. She may decide to postpone the wedding to give them time to re-adjust to the new situation. She may decide it is better to have made the mistake of getting engaged rather than to make the mistake of getting married. Then again, she may decide that her fears are groundless. In that eventually, both partners will now have a far deeper understanding of each other.

Supporting your wife

With all the attention focused on your daughter, it is all too easy to forget what a massive day this is for her mother too. Like you, your wife is certain to be experiencing a crazy cocktail of often contradictory emotions. Along with the pleasure she is hopefully feeling, there's bound to be a lot of spoken and unspoken nostalgia in the air. After all, this is the day that begins the transition from her little girl to someone's wife.

This rite of passage can be an incredibly difficult time for mother and daughter alike. It's a push and pull that quite probably will not end until well into your daughter's first year of marriage. It's only at that stage that she probably will begin to feel comfortable enough with her new status that she no longer needs to continually remind everyone that she really is an independent, married woman.

And if the wedding involves divorced and/or remarried parents, relatives who at best tolerate each other, and perhaps even a son-in-law she does not even like, the stress levels can be off the scale.

And if all this isn't enough for her to have to handle, how must she be thinking now you and your daughter will be in the spotlight as she's pushed to one side? She may well have been involved in all the wedding planning, but now tradition decrees that *you* will accompany your daughter to the church, *you* will walk her down the aisle, *you* will hand her over to her new husband, *you* will make that emotional speech and *you* will dance with her at the reception.

Of course, you *should* have been discussing all these emotional and logistical issues with your wife for months, if not for years. Whether you have or not, you certainly need to now.

Talk and be affectionate

She is probably as nervous and uptight as your daughter, maybe more so. What if the car doesn't turn up? What if the chef is unwell? What if Uncle Steve drinks too much? What if...? What if...? What if...? Reassure her that you have contingency plans. Ask her *if* and *how* you can help. Does she need any last minute shopping? Are there any phone calls to be made? Tell your wife what a fantastic job she has done, not only over the last few months, but over your daughter's entire lifetime – and mean it.

Whatever you do, don't allow either of you to lose sight of the romance that surrounds the day. Remind her of *your* wedding day. Talk, hold hands, dance. Tell her what a wonderful wife and mother she is and pay her genuine compliments: 'You shouldn't look so beautiful; it isn't fair on the bride.'

Stress busting

While this is a day for the entire family, everyone involved will benefit from a few quiet time-outs throughout the proceedings.

Here are a few relaxation techniques that can really help when you feel the pressure is getting to you:

▶ **The hammock**

Imagine you have been walking along a beach for hours. You are very tired. Suddenly you spot a hammock at the top of a steep sand dune. You begin to climb the dune, but you are now becoming more exhausted. *Only ten more steps to go, now nine*... you can hardly stand up... *now eight, seven, six*... feel the agony of each step upwards *five, four, three*...not far...now *two, one*, you make it! Collapse into the hammock and relax completely.

▶ **The great outdoors**

Picture yourself sitting next to a campfire. Every time you have a negative thought, imagine it gently drifting away from you in a puff of smoke. If you prefer, see yourself relaxing on a river bank with your tensions, fears and anxieties inside logs which are serenely floating away from you.

▶ **Your favourite place**

Visit you favourite place – real or imagined, past, present or future. This is your very own secret place, and because it is in your mind's eye, no-one else need ever know about it. Perhaps it is a beautiful valley with a small river flowing through it. Use all your senses – *see* the blue sky, *hear* the gurgling stream, *smell* the scented flowers, *taste* the cool water, *touch* the warm grass. Really *be there*. Remain in your favourite place until you are perfectly relaxed and ready to return to the bustle of the real world.

These techniques may sound silly to you, but they are not, for one simple reason – they work.

Getting her to the church (almost) on time

After confirming that the cars have arrived as arranged to take the bridesmaids, the mother of the bride and other members of the family to the ceremony, help your daughter into her wedding car (or whatever mode of transport is being utilised), making sure her dress is not crushed.

This is probably the only time you'll spend alone with your daughter all day, so make the most of it. Try to respond to her emotional state. She may wish to talk or may simply hold your hand in silence. If she's happy, that's wonderful. If she's nervous or sad, reassure her that things will be fine. Crack a joke or two to lighten the mood, so long as it doesn't annoy her. Even if she seems to be totally irrational, never argue or lose your temper. This is a day for unconditional support.

Bear in mind she's likely to be very nervous, so any words of comfort or wisdom you can offer will be appreciated. Have a few tissues handy too. She might need some – and so might you. As you arrive at the wedding site, seize the moment and say something simple, sincere and significant: 'You'll remember this moment for the rest of your life.'

YOUR DUTIES AT THE CEREMONY

While your daughter, of course, is the star of the show, for the next few minutes you will also be taking centre stage. Try to relax and enjoy the moment – and encourage her to do the same.

Walking up the aisle

Traditionally, you stand with your daughter at the back and enter when the music begins. You are then followed by your daughter's entourage. Nowadays, however, many brides reverse the order of entry, following the American pattern. Perhaps the flower girls will enter first, followed by the bridesmaids and ushers. Only once everyone else is seated, do you and your daughter make your dramatic entrance.

If your daughter prefers this variation, she needs to choose the right music. It could seem somewhat bizarre for two three year old girls to enter to the accompaniment of *Here Comes the Bride*.

Stand to your daughter's right, arm in arm. As you walk down the aisle – or escort her into the register office or into any of the legally 'approved premises' – smile and nod to guests but concentrate mostly upon your daughter. This is another golden opportunity to say something heartfelt and memorable: 'Love one another and you will be happy. It's as simple and as difficult as that.'

Giving the bride away

If the marriage is taking place in a church, a hymn is usually sung once you have walked your daughter down the aisle. The vicar then states the reason for the gathering and asks if anyone knows of any reason why the marriage should not take place.

Having received the couple's agreement to be married, the vicar asks who is giving the bride away. The bride hands her bouquet to the chief bridesmaid and you place your daughter's right hand in that of the vicar, who gives it to the groom. The symbolism of this moment is clear and poignant. Your little girl is becoming a woman and you are passing responsibility for her to another. So don't just turn her in the general direction of the groom and scamper off to your seat. Make eye contact with both of them, smile, shake his hand firmly, give him a word of encouragement – and kiss your daughter. *Now* you can sit.

After the ceremony

Once vows and rings have been exchanged, the bride and groom lead the way to sign the register. They then walk back down the aisle, followed by the chief bridesmaid with the best man; any other attendants; the bride's mother with the groom's father; and the groom's mother with you at her right-hand side.

The party then poses for the wedding pictures. Be guided here by the professional photographer who will know how to get the best results. This is a time to relax and chat with family and friends. Then everyone moves on to the reception. Traditionally, you accompany the groom's mother, usually in the third car – following the bridesmaids and the best man. If there are only two official cars, you may decide to use your own vehicle, with your wife and the groom's parents as passengers.

Reception Responsibilities 10

'I awoke this morning with devout thanksgiving for my friends, the old and the new.' (Ralph Waldo Emerson)

It's party time!

Whether it's a drinks and dinner do, an evening event, an afternoon only affair, an evening buffet, or some other arrangement, you'll have some important duties to perform. As always, be prepared to be flexible, given your family circumstances and your daughter's wishes.

However formal the occasion, please don't spend so much time fretting about your obligations that you forget to enjoy yourself. Remember, without you there may not have been such a wonderful wedding – or, come to think of it, even a bride. Take time out to relax, chat to people and accept compliments.

Get the ushers involved to give you more 'quality time' with your immediate family. And keep things in perspective. Perfection is of no consequence, logistical mishaps are trivial and unimportant. If anything does go a little awry, it will probably go down as a humorous and treasured family memory.

BEING THE HOST WITH THE MOST
Whether you are the official host of the reception or technically a guest, your daughter is certain to appreciate your help and support

during the festivities. It's tricky to find the right balance. Do you continually rush round making sure everyone is enjoying themselves, or do you make a few introductions and then throw caution to the wind allowing them get on with it? To make sure you don't end up at either extreme, consider the following advice and strategies.

Greeting the guests

Traditionally there is a receiving line to greet the guests as they arrive at the reception or as they enter the room for the wedding breakfast. The bride's mother should be first in line, followed by you and then *possibly* by other members of the wedding party. Etiquette is open to interpretation on that one.

The disadvantage of this procedure, especially at a big wedding, is that it can take an age to make small talk with every single guest. The newlyweds may prefer to welcome the guests on their own, or alongside the toastmaster or catering manager, leaving you to mingle, circulate, smile and make introductions.

An alternative arrangement would be for the bride and groom to make a triumphal entry *after* all the guests have arrived. As they enter, they are then greeted with a chorus of clapping, cheering, whistling and camera flashes.

Mood music

Atmosphere is important. You need to start on the right note. Whether it's recorded or live, background music helps set just the right mood and gets guests ready to celebrate. 'Background' is the key word here. Your guests will be chatting, so keep the volume down. If funds permit consider a string quartet or jazz band, to add a sophisticated touch.

Drinks

It is always a nice touch to offer your guests a welcome drink as they arrive. While a glass of bubbly is the traditional wedding beverage, remember that people may prefer something non-alcoholic, to start with at least. It's not necessary to wait on them hand and foot. Pour their *first* drink. Let everyone know where they can find refills. You really don't need to circle the room checking guests have a full glass.

Getting the seating plan right

Perhaps your daughter wants the traditional seating arrangement of a top table, comprising the bridal couple and immediate bridal party, with closer friends and relatives sitting at the closest tables. Or maybe she would prefer people spread about with no obvious pecking order. The important thing is to think about who would enjoy conversing together, even if they don't (yet) know each other – and, equally importantly, who would most certainly *not* enjoy sitting together.

If you want to avoid hearing the likes of: 'I'm only on Table 7, while *she's* on Table 3', give the tables names rather than numbers. Suitable names would be ones associated with the theme of the occasion (if there is one), or perhaps words for love in various languages.

Let me entertain you

Think carefully about *what sort* of entertainment will be provided. You don't need to fill every minute but one or two fun activities during the reception are sure to go down well. It really is a case of less is more. You also need to consider *when* you'll want to provide a little fun and games. Perhaps it is during the 'quiet' period between dinner and dancing.

Activities that require concentration for long periods of time, like board games or quizzes, are best confined to smaller gatherings, while the all-pervading noise of karaoke all afternoon or evening will grate on people's nerves, especially if the person holding the microphone can't sing. That said, there may be a case for a little bellowing towards the end of proceedings.

Physical activities are often the best way of breaking the ice between people who aren't great at small talk. If you've got the space – and the budget – try something everybody can have a go at, such as having a little flutter at a mini casino. Companies bring everything they need with them, from chips and croupiers to fun money and dice. Other options include caricaturists, silhouette artists and magicians.

Involving the guests

The best sort of party entertainment gets people actively involved, *if they want to.* Don't organise anything that would be intrusive for people who aren't interested in participating. Think of a novel idea or two which will add an element of fun to the function or include an activity to *encourage* your guests to interact. The opportunities are endless. Here are a just few touches that can help make the reception unique, personal and memorable:

► **Video diary**

Set up a *Big Brother*-like video diary room where guests can leave personal messages.

► **Dedications**

Include a 'dedication form' with each invitation and get the DJ to read them out (and play the songs).

▶ **Photoboard**

Provide some photos of your daughter (and son-in-law) as babies, children and young adults. Alternatively, provide some old photos of each member of the wedding party and challenge the guests to decide who's who.

▶ **Speech sweepstake**

Guess the length of the best man's speech. Winner takes all.

▶ **Disposable cameras**

Leave one or two on each table and encourage guests to click away at will. Another idea is to include Post-it notes with the cameras. Guests can write funny or serious captions that relate to the moment and these can be included in an album once the photos are developed.

▶ **Varying the drinks**

Put (or arrange for) a different combination of drinks on each table (red wines, white wines, lagers, alcopops, mineral waters, fruit juices). This will encourage cross table interaction as people barter and swap bottles and jugs.

▶ **Poetic licence**

Invite each table to compose a poem, complete a limerick or propose a toast to be read out (after any necessary censorship) by the best man.

▶ **Raffle**

Make a draw to decide who takes home the various table centres (and possibly the floral arrangements).

▶ **Chocolate fountains**

These have become very popular recently. However, it is important to appreciate the practicality of cramming a large number of guests around a single fountain. And of course, things can get a little messy if there are a lot of children present.

Don't forget the children

Younger children in particular will soon become bored and potentially disruptive if they are expected to sit though a series of speeches and a seemingly endless number of photo opportunities. If you plan a few activities especially for them, *everyone's* day will be much more enjoyable – and peaceful. Here are some possibilities:

- ▶ Hire a professional nursery nurse.
- ▶ Book a children's entertainer.
- ▶ Arrange a treasure hunt.
- ▶ Provide goody bags.
- ▶ Provide a craft area where they can have fun and get creative.
- ▶ Ask them to draw pictures of the wedding.
- ▶ Show them a kiddies' DVD.
- ▶ Give them a quiet place where they can 'de-hype'.

Surprise, surprise?

You may decide to give the happy couple – and the guests in general – a little surprise at the reception. Here's one idea to ponder. During the canapés, hand out balloons with postcards on the bottom and ask everyone to write a personal note on the stamped addressed card. Invite everyone outside and release the balloons.

For the next few months the newlyweds should be receiving cards from all over the country and possibly from overseas. To make it more competitive (and to encourage people to return the cards), you could offer some wine to the guest whose card travelled the furthest and some euros to the person who returned it. What's great about this surprise is that it keeps the memory of the wedding alive for weeks, during a time which can sometimes seem a little flat.

MAKING THE FIRST SPEECH

Some couples will decide to have the speeches *before* the meal. This allows nervous speakers to get their speeches 'out of the way' so they can relax and enjoy the occasion. Most toastmasters and other wedding advisers counsel against this as tight catering schedules can be severely disrupted if speeches go on for longer than intended. Also, if there is no obvious highlight at the end of the meal, things can tend to peter out as individuals and groups of people migrate to the bar and elsewhere.

For these reasons, it is traditional for the speeches to take place *after* people have eaten. It is important to know who is going to speak, and in what order. It is usual for the bride's father to speak first, especially if he is hosting the event.

Fortunately the guests will understand what an emotional day this is for you. They will be on your side and willing you to do well, so try to enjoy the limelight. Quite frankly, they won't give a damn if you fluff a line or two. All they want is to experience a genuine, sensitive, heartfelt speech. Every father wants to do his daughter proud and there can be no greater compliment than expressing his feelings in an eloquent and well-presented manner.

Finding your style

It is exceedingly difficult to discuss style and technique in general terms, since the ability to 'hold an audience', to be sober, sensible, and yet amusing is such a personal business. However, there are certain 'rules' and guidelines which appear to be universal. Here they are.

Making the speech 'yours'

Did Elvis, Sinatra and Johnny Rotten all sound the same singing *My Way*? Of course not. The artist makes the crucial difference. So, too, does the speaker. Whatever individual characteristics you have that are special to you should be nurtured and cultivated and worked on, for it is those personal and unique quirks of appearance, personality and expression that will mark you out as a speaker with something different to offer. And that is never a bad thing.

Being passionate

What makes the difference between a speech that is remembered and one that has great content but is soon forgotten? It is the passion, purpose and personality that make the difference. You do not need to be an erudite, charismatic orator, but you do need to display genuine conviction, devotion and love.

If you have the burning desire to tell someone about something, you will have the enthusiasm necessary to do so and you'll find just the right words to express yourself. Tell the truth and speak from the heart. But the other side of speaking from the heart is listening to what your heart is calling you to say. The audience must believe that you believe. They will believe you only if you believe you.

Connecting with your audience

The writer E.M. Forster's mantra was: 'Only connect'. There is a huge difference between *impressing* an audience and *connecting* with them. The guests must be *certain* that you are sharing your innermost feelings – that you feel the truth of the subject, physically, emotionally, spiritually. They need to know you are breaking through clichés and moving into profound territory.

The ultimate connection is when you make each of them feel you are speaking *just to them*. In a vicarious way, they share *your* emotions, your memories, your experiences. At the same time, they silently contemplate *their* related emotions, their memories, their experiences.

The subject has become larger than itself. It has become a window into our world, an excuse for reflecting upon the most significant matters of the human experience. A bridge has been built, a bond forged. It is a wonderful feeling because an invisible chain now links every person in the room, regardless of age, gender, race, background or creed.

Being conversational

Sitting at leisure, with family, friends or colleagues, your conversation will be naturally relaxed and chatty, because that is the language of easy communication. When you make your speech, the words and phrases you use should be more considered, imaginative, creative and rhythmical than your everyday language, yet the way you say them, the way you deliver your speech, should remain unaffectedly relaxed and chatty. Certainly you may need to speak a little louder or make other concessions to accommodate the needs of your audience, but, in essence, nothing in your delivery style should change.

Casual conversation is not structured in a literary way. You do not always finish your sentences. You repeat yourself. You use ungrammatical constructions – but you are obeying a different set of rules. You are obeying the rules of effective spoken communication which have been learnt, instinctively, down the ages. Don't abandon these rules when you speak in public. Talk to your audience just as you would to John and Jane Smith. What is the audience, after all, but a collection of John and Jane Smiths?

Being heard
You must be *audible*. If you are not, all else is lost. If there is a microphone available, get as much practice as you can and then use it. If there is no sound-enhancing equipment, speak as clearly and as loudly as is necessary to be heard. If the only other person in the room was at the back, you would talk to him or her naturally, at the right level, without shouting or straining, by:

- ▶ keeping your head up
- ▶ opening your mouth wider than usual
- ▶ using clearer consonants
- ▶ slowing down.

If you remember that you must be heard by that same person, at the back, during your speech, however many other people may be in the room, you will make those same four *natural* adjustments to your delivery.

Giving out the right non-verbal messages
We *speak* with our **vocal cords**, but we *communicate* with our **whole body**. An audience does a lot more than *listen* to a speech – they *experience* it. Everything about a speaker's manner and demeanour contributes to the overall impression that the audience takes away.

So what hidden messages do you give out when you speak? If you are unsure, watch yourself in a mirror. Better still, get someone to record you. You may find that you need to work on one or more of the following. While each of these aspects of body language can be considered in isolation, a positive change made to any of them will also have a direct and immediate positive effect on the others.

Stance and posture

An aligned, upright posture conveys a message of confidence and integrity. Stand upright with your feet shoulder-width apart and very slightly turned out. You can then shift your weight from one side to the other, if you have to, without being noticed. Keep well clear of the table; leaning on it would make you look aggressive, and you could end up crying over spilt champagne. On the other hand, you may decide to walk about the room, moving among the guests as you give your address. If you take this approach, make sure you are near the right table when you talk to or about anyone directly.

Don't put your hands in your pockets or grasp them unnaturally at your back or front. Either hold any script or cue card in one hand or place it on the table in front of you. This allows you to glance at it from time to time while still giving you the freedom to use your hands to help express yourself.

Movement and gestures

Try to identify any annoying movements or gestures which you display. Aim to eliminate these because such habits are a powerful means of distraction. Your audience will become preoccupied with them and will start *watching* you rather than *listening* to you and generally *experiencing* your speech.

Eye contact and facial expression

These are crucial aspects of effective communication because they gain and maintain an audience's attention and create rapport. Try to look around the room and from time to time focus on those guests who are furthest away. Include everyone as you speak. It is all too easy to end up having a private chat to the people closest to you.

However you must do more than simply look at your audience; you must use your eyes and your facial expression to help convey your *feelings*. This is not as difficult as it may sound. You do it every day. If you genuinely believe in what you are saying, your emotions will be revealed naturally through your eyes and your expression.

There is nothing more captivating than a smile. It shows a warmth and friendliness and says, 'I'm really pleased to be making this speech.' So smile, smile – and then smile again.

Once you begin to give out these positive silent messages about your feelings and emotions, you will become even more enthusiastic and eager – and this, in turn, will be reflected in your body language. You will have broken into a wonderful, virtuous circle.

Thinking positively

Tell yourself you are going to make a great speech. And *believe* it. The largely untapped power of positive thinking really is immense. It has been estimated that 85% of performance is directly related to *attitude*. Unfortunately, many speakers think they are going to struggle, and this becomes a self-fulfilling prophesy. As Henry Ford put it: 'Whether you think you will succeed or whether you think you will fail, you will probably be right.'

Visualising success

Visualisation is the planting of mental images into the subconscious mind. These images have to be vivid and real – you must be able to *see*, to *hear*, to *smell*, to *touch*, to *taste* – and to truly *live them*.

When you can *imagine* an event over which you have some control happening, it will greatly increase the likelihood of it *actually* happening. This is not a crankish idea. Controlled medical experiments have proved it to be true.

You are now going to watch a film clip with a difference – because the screenwriter, the director, the cameraman and the star will be *you*. Close your eyes and visualise yourself rising to speak. You are looking good. Feel the warmth of the audience. You are surrounded by family and friends. You pause for a moment and then begin. They love your opening hook. But it gets better; your touching reminiscences and occasional jokes wow them. Laughter one moment, tears the next. They are eating out of your hand. Then comes that emotion-packed big finish, your verbal final round knock out. Nobody could have topped that. Listen to their cheers and applause. Now that's what I call a wedding speech!

Making fear your friend
Even the best-prepared and psyched-up speaker can suffer from a sudden attack of the collywobbles. It is perfectly natural and normal to feel a *little* nervous before delivering a speech. In fact, it helps if you do. The adrenalin will flow and you will be charged up and ready to give a really great performance.

However, if you feel *too* nervous, the quality of your speech will suffer. As you sit there, remind yourself that the audience are not a jury. They will readily forgive any little gaffs so long as you are genuine and sincere in everything you say. Remember that 90% of nervousness is internal; only 10% displays itself to the outside world. You may feel shaky as you wait to be introduced, but the guests won't know that – unless you tell them. So *never* tell them.

Whatever you do, don't drink too much. Booze is like success, it is great until it goes to your head. As the late, great Bob Monkhouse used to say: 'Never accept a drink before you speak; never refuse one after.'

Meeting the guests

Try to talk to, or at least shake hands and exchange pleasantries with, as many guests as possible before you speak, especially people you do not know. This will have a calming influence on you as you will then not be talking to total strangers. Make one or two passing references to some of these people as you speak – but make sure you get their names right. If you do this, the whole of the groom's family and friends will feel far more included and your speech will come over as conversational, friendly and spontaneous.

Emergency relaxation techniques

If the pressure is really starting to get to you, try one or two of these pre-speech emergency relaxation techniques. They can be used anywhere and any time without anyone, except you, knowing it.

Stopping negative thoughts

1. Tell yourself: Stop!
2. Breathe in and hold your breath.
3. Exhale slowly, relaxing your shoulders and hands.
4. Pause, breathe in slowly, relaxing your forehead and jaw.
5. Remain quiet and still for a few moments.

Sitting at a table

1. Pull in your stomach muscles tightly, relax.
2. Clench your fists tightly, relax.
3. Grasp the seat of your chair, relax.
4. Press your elbows tightly into the sides of your body, relax.
5. Push your feet into the floor, relax.

Spot relaxation

1. Imagine your shoulders are very heavy.
2. Hunch them up.
3. Drop them down slowly.
4. Gently tip your head forward and feel the muscles pulling up through the middle of your shoulder blades.
5. Move your head gently backwards and feel the tension in the muscles down the front of your neck.
6. Bring your head back to an upright position and breathe in very deeply for a few moments.

Coping during your speech

Most people's nerves will evaporate once they are introduced and they begin to speak. Think about it this way: most footballers feel nervous, especially before a big game. But once they hear the shrill of the first whistle, their nerves seem to disappear. The reason? At that moment all their pent up tension is released and they can finally get on with the job in hand.

If you are still feeling a little jittery as you begin your address, these tips will help you cope:

▶ Smile naturally and find a few particularly friendly faces. Maintain plenty of eye contact with them. As your confidence grows, look more and more at other people around the rest of the room.

▶ Never admit that you are the slightest bit nervous.

▶ Keep your notes on the table so they can't be heard rattling, be seen shaking or end up all over the floor.

▶ Don't draw attention to your hands.

▶ Don't hold a hand-mike. Leave it on its stand.

▶ If your mouth feels dry and your throat tightens up, take a sip of water.

However, always remember that the greatest antidotes to nerves are preparation and attitude. If you prepare well and have a positive attitude, what used to be called fear can be re-named excitement and anticipation.

DANCING THE NIGHT AWAY

Assuming that you are physically fit to do so, it is usual for the father of the bride to be involved in at least some of the dances. You could go to lessons or buy a DVD. Then again, you may decide to just shuffle around the floor, smiling and chatting. After all, it's not *Strictly Come Dancing* so you're not going to be slated by Craig Revel Horwood and the gang.

Being involved in the first dance

The first dance is usually announced by the band or DJ and it is taken as the official start of the evening reception. The groom escorts his bride onto the floor and after a chorus or two they are joined by the rest of the immediate wedding party. It is traditional for you to dance with the groom's mother. After a few more bars, you are joined by the rest of the guests.

Sharing the father-daughter dance

Whether you and your daughter are as graceful as Fred and Ginger – or as ungainly as Fred and Wilma – this can be a genuinely touching moment as you take the floor together for the second dance. And if you've secretly worked out a dance routine together, this can bring the house down.

It is important for you both to choose the right song. It should be meaningful to each of you, but the lyrics should also be appropriate to the occasion. While your selection should be personal, look for something memorable and inspiring; something that will melt the heart of daughter, father – and each and every onlooker. Here are just a dozen possibilities, any of which would be sure to go down well:

- ► My Little Girl (Tim McGraw)
- ► I Loved Her First (Heartland)
- ► In My Daughter's Eyes (Martina McBride)
- ► Butterfly Kisses (Bob Carlisle)
- ► Through the Years (Kenny Rogers)
- ► To Dance with My Father Again (Luther Vandross)
- ► Sunrise, Sunset (Topol, Miriam Karlin and Company; *Fiddler on the Roof*) (Choose this one only if the groom is tall)
- ► Lullabye (Goodnight My Angel) (Billy Joel)
- ► My Girl (The Temptations)
- ► Father and Daughter (Paul Simon)
- ► The Way You Look Tonight (Frank Sinatra)
- ► Unforgettable (Nat and Natalie Cole)

If some of these songs are new to you, it is well worth checking them out first on YouTube.

Into the groove

At this stage the volume and tempo will be revved up to bring guests onto their feet. Almost everyone will get up to dance at a wedding, especially after consuming a glass or two. While the actual playlist must be a personal choice, here is a selection of some classy and some cheesy dance songs which would be certain to get the party swinging. They span over fifty years and are listed in the order they were released (or, in some cases, some might argue, the order they escaped):

- ▶ Rock Around the Clock (Bill Haley and His Comets)
- ▶ Twist and Shout (The Beatles)
- ▶ Oops Upside Your Head (The Gap Band)
- ▶ Do the Conga (Black Lace)
- ▶ Locomotion (Kylie Minogue)
- ▶ The Only Way is Up (Yazz and the Plastic Population)
- ▶ Cotton Eye Joe (Rednex)
- ▶ Macarena (Los del Rio)
- ▶ Dance the Night Away (The Mavericks)
- ▶ We Like to Party (Vengaboys)
- ▶ Reach (S Club 7)
- ▶ Mercy (Duffy).

Encourage your daughter to choose a wide range of music that will include something for everyone. That means playing something by the Andrew Sisters as well as the Scissor Sisters; something by Glenn Miller as well as Steve Miller.

Getting people involved in the last dance

These days everyone gets involved in the final dance, singing and possibly linking arms or forming a circle around the newlyweds. This makes for a great climax as the happy couple are given a memorable send-off. Some favourites for this 'big finish' are:

- All You Need is Love (The Beatles)
- You'll Never Walk Alone (Gerry and the Pacemakers)
- Angels (Robbie Williams)
- Hi Ho Silver Lining (Jeff Beck)
- Auld Lang Syne (Traditional)
- Congratulations (Cliff Richard)
- Glad All Over (Dave Clark Five)
- I've Had The Time of My Life (Bill Medley & Jennifer Warnes)
- New York, New York (Frank Sinatra)
- That's Amore (Dean Martin)
- Viva Las Vegas (Elvis Presley)
- Walking On Sunshine (Katrina & the Waves).

The bottom line

While people will appreciate well-presented food, drink and entertainment, the biggest factor in any reception's success is the welfare and enjoyment of the guests. Don't confine your attentions to the big groups of people who are obviously already having a good time. Take a good look around the room and see whether anybody's struggling to get a conversation going, or standing shyly on the sidelines. Go over and take the pressure off them by initiating a discussion, introducing timid types to other people or suggesting they check out the entertainment on offer.

Keep a close eye out for any youngsters who may be drinking too much and any elderly guests who may be flagging. Don't allow the wedding breakfast to become a dog's dinner. If a problem arises, remind yourself that it will *not* be a turning point in the history of

Western civilisation. Relax, smile and quietly sort it out without interrupting anybody else's fun. The golden rule of reception hosting is never panic!

The grand finale

Traditionally, the bride and groom will have left the reception shortly before the final dance. However, this does not always happen nowadays with some newlyweds partying on until the celebration ends.

People may leave the reception at different times. As host, you should escort them to the door and check they've picked up their coats. *Tell* them you hope they've had a good time. This is far better than fishing for compliments by *asking* if they've enjoyed themselves.

Aim to end proceedings on a high rather than allowing things to fizzle out. When you sense the moment is right, consult with your daughter and her new husband and then announce that final dance.

The Future 11

'I'm letting go, but I'll never be far.
You can always reach me, wherever you are.
I watch you proudly as you start on your way.
My love goes with you as we start a new day.' (Pearl Simmons)

There's always a moment during the wedding day when it hits you. The gravitas may impact as you walk down the aisle, as you leave the church, as you dance with your daughter. Whenever and wherever it may happen, be totally assured that it *will* happen.

RIDING THAT EMOTIONAL ROLLER COASTER

Throughout the day both of you will walk that delicate line between past and future. During this bittersweet transitional period your emotions will include everything from anxiety to hope, guilt to pride, fear to relief. You will be experiencing all the inevitable and often contradictory physical and emotional processes of letting go. And letting go is never easy.

Should you express every emotion you are experiencing? Well, you certainly shouldn't bottle things up; it's fine to acknowledge publicly how you feel – with measured restraint. You need to be expressive without ever becoming *overly* emotional. If you have ignored your feelings until today, put off *really* expressing them until tomorrow. Your daughter is happy. Allow her to be happy.

The important thing is to understand that what you're feeling is normal, and that you are not the only father who has moments when he wishes he could turn back the clock and perhaps do one or two things differently.

For worse or for better?

When the last glass of champagne has been drunk, and the final guest has left, in a moment of silent reflection you will understand that your life can never be quite the same again. But a *different* life does not necessarily mean a *worse* life. If you act wisely and judiciously, this may be the beginning of an even stronger relationship between the two of you.

TAKING A BACK SEAT

Even if your daughter has been living independently for years, things change fundamentally when she speaks those small, massive words: 'I do.' At that instant her priorities shift. Her husband becomes the main person in her life. You have to accept this.

Remember that while you will remain *her* father, you will now become *his* father-in-law. If you don't want to get the reputation of being a meddling old busybody, you need to stay out of their marriage as much as is humanly possible. You need to maintain a literal and metaphorical distance.

To dream the impossible dream

Did you always have the hope and even the expectation that your daughter would be given opportunities to do things and go places you never did? Was your secret ambition that one day she would live your dreams? It can't be easy, but you have to realise that this is now unlikely to happen. She has become a married woman now and it is *their* individual and collective goals that count.

It is quite possible that your daughter's own lifelong dreams have also been cast aside in favour of more pressing domestic commitments. Such decisions cannot have been easy for her. Whatever you feel about this, you have to trust her judgment and accept her priorities. The wisest fathers know that if they can't say anything pleasant and supportive, they shouldn't say anything at all.

THE HONEYMOON PERIOD IS OVER

After the honeymoon your daughter will be re-joining the real world and that can sometimes be a very difficult re-adjustment. Some brides seem totally unwilling or unable to accept that they cannot continue to live a fairy story lifestyle, while others find the realities of their new everyday life to be a terrible anti-climax after all the razzmatazz of their dream wedding. Both extremes are highly undesirable. As her father, you may be able to help resolve matters, so long as you act responsibly and tactfully.

Dream on

When she returns from her sun-kissed honeymoon, she seems a little *too* happy to you. She simply refuses to allow anyone to prick her fairy tale bubble. This magical, dream-like existence will go on forever. As a parent, with a few years experience behind you, you know it won't. Bills will need to be paid, repairs will need to be made, problems will need to be resolved. It's only a matter of time before the walls of her fantasy kingdom come crashing down around her, or directly on top of her. That is when you'll need to be there to pick up the pieces. Until that day arrives, hold your tongue and allow her to live in her wonderful world of naive wedded bliss.

Post-wedding blues

The confetti has been thrown, the cake eaten and the dress folded away, but for some brides the start of married life marks the start of a depression, leaving sufferers feeling disillusioned, confused and even questioning whether getting married was a mistake.

Today one in ten brides falls prey to a condition known as Post-Nuptial Depression, which makes them feel desperately low, aimless and disconnected from their newly married status. To them, life after the wedding seems mundane and meaningless with nothing to look forward to. In severe cases the black cloud can linger for up to a year, making for a miserable start to married life.

The condition stems from the belief that marriage will somehow elevate couples to a higher and somehow happier state of existence. The sometimes boring day-to-day actuality can lead to problems, especially after months of being the centre of attention and possibly being indulged and spoiled. The reality is that a wedding is the start of a special relationship but, all too often, a bride's focus is on the *day* and not the *years ahead*.

Support her
This can be a difficult time and you do not want to aggravate things by being ham-fisted. However, there are some subtle ways of helping her. Firstly, you could tell her in advance that she may suffer from this post-wedding reaction. It is perfectly normal and it will pass. Feeling married and behaving married takes time. It is an attitude; a way of being that grows and develops.

She needs a period of adjustment. Help her to come down gently from the high of her wedding. You could arrange some social events so she has something to look forward to after the honeymoon. Invite lots of her friends, too. It is important that she does not ignore, and possibly lose, her close network of companions.

Because she has to get used to no longer always being the centre of attraction, it is best to arrange gatherings around external events, such as a Wimbledon tennis final, or an Oscars evening. Alternatively, throw a birthday or graduation party for someone else. Suggest that the newlyweds and you oldlyweds meet regularly, once a month, for a meal or an evening out. Avoid wedding talk. Discuss what they are doing *now* and what they are planning for the *future*.

A GIRL ALWAYS NEEDS HER FATHER

Of course, your daughter still loves you. A girl's dad can never be replaced and will always remain in her heart. She has simply begun a new chapter in her life. And so have you. As you let her go, you can be certain that she *will* come back to you. It's like holding quicksilver in your hand: leave your fingers open and it stays, clutch it and it darts away.

That gap-toothed little girl has become a woman. By encouraging independence within her marriage, you'll be opening up a doorway to an even richer, deeper understanding of each other – and a lifelong relationship to match.

Life goes on

Perhaps watching the two of them together reminds you so much of her mother and you at their age, when your love was new and tender. Where did the years go? Why, it wasn't so long ago that *you* were the young lovers, then the young parents, working together to make a life. Switch your attention from your daughter to her mother, who will need your love, comfort and support. She too is facing a new situation without her daughter. However, she still has you – and you still have her. Marriage is like wine; it gets better with age.

Well that's about it, Dad. What a journey it's been. It's possibly been expensive; it's probably been hard work; it's *definitely* been worth it. Pour yourself a mug of Dom Perignon. You deserve it.

Resources

Here is a selection of books and websites which should prove of interest and value both to fathers of the bride and their daughters.

MARRIAGE PREPARATION
Rules of Engagement, Richard and Katharine Hill (Lion Hudson and Care for the Family).

ON MARRIAGE
The Sixty Minute Marriage, Rob Parsons (Hodder and Stoughton).
The Marriage Book, Nicky and Sila Lee (Alpha International Publications).
The Highway Code of Marriage, Michael and Hilary Perrott (CWR).
The Five Love Languages, Gary Chapman (Northfield Publishing).
The Seven Principles for Making Marriage Work, John Gottman (Crown Publishers).
Why Marriages Succeed or Fail, John Gottman (Simon and Schuster).

www.2-in2-1.co.uk
www.careforthefamily.org.uk
www.foccus.co.uk
www.themarriagecourse.org

PLANNING A WEDDING
Get Wed For Less, Elizabeth Catherine Myers (How To Books).
How to Get Married in Green, Susan St Maur (How To Books).

Wedding Planner, Elizabeth Catherine Myers (How To Books).
Wedding Secrets, Tamryn Kirby (Foulsham).

www.confetti.co.uk
www.hitched.co.uk
www.wedddingguide.co.uk

CHURCH WEDDINGS

To find all the requirements and procedures for getting married in church, see:

www.findachurch.co.uk

CIVIL CEREMONIES

If it's going to be a civil ceremony, the most informative site is:

www.registerofficeweddings.com

Approved premises

The Marriages Act (1994) has permitted civil marriages to take place outside register offices. Other venues can now be licensed to allow civil ceremonies to be performed there. There are thousands of registered venues throughout England and Wales.

For a full list of approved premises, visit:

www.statistics.gov.uk/registration/premises

Follow the links and then type in the postcode, town or county to get details of all the venues available in any particular area.

To purchase a hard copy of the current venue directory, write to:

Local Services
General Register Office
PO Box 56
Southport
PR8 2GL

You will need to enclose a cheque or postal order for £10.00, made payable to 'GRO' (General Register Office).

Credit/debit card orders can be made by telephoning 0151 471 4817.

CIVIL PARTNERSHIPS

Although, legally speaking, they are not 'weddings', civil partnership ceremonies are similar to civil weddings. For more details, log on to:

www.civilpartnerships.org.uk

SPECIFIC FAITHS AND CULTURES

In our multicultural society, interfaith marriages are becoming more and more common. A good general site which includes discussion on related issues is:

www.interfaithmarriage.co.uk

If you want to find out more about the beliefs and traditions of a specific faith or culture, visit the relevant site:

Hindu
www.lalwani.demon.co.uk/sonney/wedding.htm

Humanist
www.humanism.org.uk/weddings

Jewish
www.beingjewish.com.cycle/wedding.html

Mormon
www.templemarriage.com

Muslim
www.mybindi.com/weddings/ceremonies/muslim/cfm

Sikh
www.sikhs.org/wedding

WEDDING SUPPLIERS

There are thousands – possibly millions – of these websites out
there. The inclusion of a particular site does *not* imply a
recommendation. Ultimately, it's down to you and the happy couple
to do a little surfing to find the most suitable ones, given your
particular circumstances and requirements.

Limousine Hire
www.american-limousines.co.uk (organised by UK postcode)
www.stretched-4-u.co.uk
www.callalimo.co.uk
www.limohiredirectory.com
www.limoshop.co.uk

Music
www.pnms.co.uk
www.mfiles.co.uk
www.gig-guide.co.uk
www.hiway.co.uk
www.excite.co.uk

Wedding Suit Hire
www.wedding-service.co.uk
www.menswear-hire.co.uk
www.countywedding.co.uk

Wedding Gifts
www.thegiftexperience.co.uk
www.bust-ed.co.uk
www.shopsafe.co.uk
www.greatgifts.org
www.coolershopping.co.uk

ADVICE ON FINANCE

The following titles were written for an American readership. However, the basic principles expounded are equally applicable in the UK.

The Newlyweds' Guide to Investing and Personal Finance, Carol L. Coqhill (Career Press).
Yes, You Can ... Achieve Financial Harmony: A newlyweds' guide to understanding money, Sam Goller and Deborah Shouse (Andrews McMeel Publishing).
Financial Bliss: How to grow wealthy together, Sarah Pennells (Prentice Hall Life).

Get a Financial Life: Personal finance in your twenties and thirties, Beth
   Kobliner (Fireside Press).

www.cheap-wedding-success.co.uk
www.moneysavingexpert.com
www.fool.co.uk

In addition to offering useful general financial advice for couples,
each of these sites also provides imaginative 'wedding on a
shoestring' strategies.

MAKING YOUR SPEECH
I must declare an interest on this one:

Making the Father of the Bride's Speech, John Bowden (How To Books).
Making a Wedding Speech, John Bowden (How to Books).

Index

abroad, marrying, *see* destination
    weddings
advice, proffering, 44, 75
    financial, 88–95
    general, 76–80
    legal, 81–8
    see also financial; legal
alcohol, *see* drinks

bridal fairs, *see* wedding fairs
bride
    adopted, 11–12
    aisle, walking up with, 147
    Bridezilla, 18–19
    children of, 15–16, 59–61
    church on time, getting to, 146
    co–habitation of, 16–18
    contributing to costs? 41–2
    dancing with, 165
    depression of, 172–3
    estranged, 12–3
    future of, 169–74
    giving away, 147–8
    last minute doubts, her, 141–2
    new wife versus, 56
    overprotection of, 6–7
    perception of, your, 3–5, 23
    pregnant, 14–15
    previous relationships of, 12
    relationship with, your, 5–7, 173–4
    remarrying, 13–14
    siblings of, 57–8
    see also support
budgeting
    discussing with bride and groom, 41–2,
        63, 68
    discussing with groom's family? 41–2,
        63
    engagement party, for, 135
    modern weddings, 41–2

prioritising, 43, 66
second/subsequent marriages, for, 14
setting a budget, 42–3, 63
traditional weddings, 40–1
see also expenses; money

catering
    engagement party, at, 130, 132, 133,
        136
    reception, at, 69–70
ceremony
    civil or religious? 82, 140
    saving money on, 69
    seating at, 54
    see also duties
challenges, possible
    bride, character, background and
        circumstances of, 11–19 *passim*
    Bridezilla, 18–19
    calling wedding off? 142–3
    competitive wedding syndrome, 19,
        42, 65–6
    estranged bride, 12–13
    groom, character, background and
        circumstances of, 20–33 *passim*
    in–laws, 79–80
    post–nuptial depression, 172–3
    pregnancy, 14–15
    religious, cultural or racial differences,
        29–30
    your character, background and
        circumstances, 8–11 *passim*
    see also bride; budgeting; children;
        expenses; family relations
children
    from bride's previous relationship(s),
        15–16, 59
    from groom's previous relationship(s),
        15–16, 26–7, 59
    keeping them amused, 154